YOUR
BIG FAT
JUICY LIFE

(AND EVERYTHING AFTER)

Published by Lisa Hagan Books 2025

www.lisahaganbooks.com

Copyright © Stephanie James 2025

ISBN: 978-1-945962-68-4

All Rights Reserved. No part of this publication may be reproduced, stored in a retrieval system, or transmitted in any form, or by any means, electronic, mechanical, photocopying, recording or otherwise without the prior permission in writing of the copyright holders, nor be otherwise circulated in any form or binding or cover other than in which it is published and without a similar condition being imposed on the subsequent publisher.

Cover photography: Tonya Thornton

Cover and interior layout by Simon Hartshorne

YOUR BIG FAT JUICY LIFE

(AND EVERYTHING AFTER)

STEPHANIE JAMES

Contents

Chapter One: The Eternal Spark ... 14
Continued Illumination ... 18
Your Immortal Soul ... 21
Tapping In: ... 24

Chapter Two: Making Peace with It All ... 25
The Peace Process ... 26
Practicing Peace ... 30
Letting Go ... 32
Befriending Your Fear ... 33
Befriending Death ... 36
Us or Them ... 39
Next Steps ... 43
Tapping In: ... 45

Chapter Three: The Divine Within ... 47
All One ... 49
The Gift of Flight ... 54
The Divine Inside ... 56
Talking to God ... 58
Tapping In: ... 59

Chapter Four: Extended Journeys ... 61
Light from Beyond ... 64
Returning to Love ... 64
The Legacy Lives On ... 67
Soul Sisters ... 73
Tapping In: ... 74

Chapter Five: We are Never Alone ... 76
The Lights at My Door ... 77
Stories From Beyond ... 81
Remembrance ... 84
What Happens Next Door ... 85
Spirit Stories ... 86
Evidence of Eternity ... 87
Tapping In: ... 90

Chapter Six: Growing Through Grief 92
Healing the Grief 94
The Importance of Connection 96
Sacred Life 98
Empowered Endings 100
Your Own Connection 104
Continued Healing 106
Tapping In: 108

Chapter Seven: Remembering the Past 110
Many Memories 116
Steve's Story 118
The Witnessing 119
Your Soul Continues 123
Tapping In: 123

Chapter Eight: Essential Interviews 125
Tapping In: 144

Chapter Nine: Connecting Past the Pain 146
The Way Things Change 149
"I'm Still Here" 153
The Connection Continues 154
Tapping in: 158

Chapter Ten: Into the Mystery 160
Coming to The End 160
The Revisiting 162
Your Journey Forward 165
Feeling Your Connection 166
The Truth in Dreams 168
Why it Matters 171
Empowered 173
Next Steps 174

Dedication

To my beautiful family, who has taught me the invaluable lesson of undying love. The joyful light, laughter, and connection we share echoes throughout eternity.

Endorsements

"Some books should be required reading for the human journey. *'Your Big Fat Juicy Life (and Everything After)'* is one that would be near the top of such a list. Stephanie James does a magnificent job of showing why death need not be feared. It is filled with wondrous stories, practical tools, and healthy perspectives about something that none of us can avoid but few want to talk about. You will want to talk about this book with others. It's a gem."
—**SUZANNE GIESEMANN,** author of *The Awakened Way – Making the Shift to a Divinely Guided Life*

"People are going to receive wonderful benefits from this joyful and deeply insightful effort. Stephanie James is a gift to us all, and this book is going to enhance the lives of its readers, extending the treasure of Who We All Are."
—**NEALE DONALD WALSCH,** modern-day spiritual messenger, author, and actor who has published 33 titles in the past 20 years, including the *Conversations with God* books

"My wholehearted gratitude for this wonderful and important book addressing perhaps our deepest fear – that of death. Through sharing profound and poignant stories of great beauty and power, it invites us to live life fully and not only to embrace death's inevitably with calmness, but realise and appreciate it as an essential step in our soul's ongoing evolutionary journey."
—**DR JUDE CURRIVAN,** cosmologist, healer, author and co-founder of *WholeWorld-View*

"A beautiful, heartfelt read, this book is more than a guide—it's a companion for anyone seeking deeper meaning and comfort along life's path. It's truly a game-changer, one that will leave you feeling nourished, inspired, and deeply grateful for every part of life's big, juicy journey."
—**ELAINE STARLING,** The Abundance Ambassador international speaker, international bestselling author, show host, and abundance coach

"*'Your Big Fat Juicy Life'* by Stephanie James is actually a love story. It not only speaks to this author's love for the true mystery and magic that is life, its many stages and truly meaningful moments and relationships, but it speaks to her love and honor for what she and the many remarkable people she includes in these pages know is not the end but, in fact, only the beginning of the next stage of the Great Mystery. Stephanie has written a book full of kind, gentle and very helpful reminders of the many things we can do to live life more fully and in this way make the transition to the next stage not only easier, but more natural, joyful, and with real wonder. I encourage you to give yourself the gift of spending quality time with this book."

—**GEORGE CAPPANNELLI,** award winning author, film & television producer, and sculptor

"This book is a profound nourishment for the soul. It's a must-read for anyone curious about life, death, the essence of the soul, and our deep connections to one another and the Divine Spark. Stephanie James masterfully shares her own journey and enriches it with enlightening interviews with other luminaries, weaving everything together with wisdom and grace. Reading this brilliant book is both comforting and uplifting—an inspiring and life-affirming experience. Put it at the top of your reading list and let it feed your soul!"

—**LISA CAMPION,** author of *The Art of Psychic Reiki*

"WOWOW! What an amazing book! I am honored to have been one of the first people to read it!! What a hope-filled book about a topic that many people can find terrifying or heartbreaking! I think Stephanie could have titled this book, How to Die Well by Living Well First. What an incredible resource to not only make peace with the death of a loved one, but a beautiful guide to prepare for the inevitable end of (this) life."

—**KAREN CURRY PARKER,** best-selling author, Human Design specialist, trainer, professional speaker, and creator of Quantum Human DesignTM and the Quantum Alignment SystemTM.

"Through the wealth of perceptive insights in her new book, *Your Big Fat Juicy Life*, Stephanie James delves into the often-forbidden topic of death with wisdom and poise, inviting the reader to explore a new perspective that both comforts and enlightens. In the book, Stephanie reveals her deep understanding of the human experience and her unwavering belief in the power of love and connection beyond the physical realm. It is a reminder that while death may be inevitable, it is not the end of our journey but rather a beautiful transition into an even greater experience. *Your Big Fat Juicy Life* is a must-read for anyone considering their own mortality or seeking consolation in the face of loss. Her message will stay with you long after you finish the final page."

—**STEVE FARRELL,** co-founder and worldwide executive director Humanity's Team

"Stephanie James' *'Your Big Fat Juicy Life'* gives voice to something that our culture desperately neglects to understand. It marks the beginning of the next timeless consciousness that is fundamental in the universe…our immortality. This book offers special healing rituals to empower us to connect deeply with our inner resources of strength, hope, and wisdom."

—**LARRY DOSSEY, MD,** author of *One Mind: How our Individual Mind is Part of A Greater Consciousness and Why It Matters, and Healing Words,* and **Barbara Dossey**, **PhD, RN,** author of *Holistic Nursing: A Handbook for Practice*

There is no escaping death. I'm going to die and you're going to die. (But don't worry. Spoiler Alert: A part of you is going to go on forever and ever and ever.) If death is something that is such a universal experience—the eventual inevitability we all face, why is it so hard for us to talk about dying? We all know that at some point in this experience we call life, there is going to be a finish line, and we, as those before us, are going to one day cross it.

This awareness can be something that drives you to do more and experience more with the limited time you have here on earth, or it can be experienced as anxiety and fear that your days are numbered and have you frantically trying to distract yourself from this reality. It can also be what leads you to dive more deeply into your spiritual life to find the meaning of it all.

As a psychotherapist, in my almost three decades of practice, I have worked with many, many people who have experienced this fear of death. Some may have just lost a loved one and some had just received a terminal diagnosis, but all of them felt they were not able to discuss death outside of my office in a way that felt safe. Some clients reported feeling that they didn't want to burden anyone with their feelings of fear, deep sadness, and anxiety. There was a feeling that these conversations were off-limits, taboo, and stifled because death is not a subject most people want to talk about.

What generates this fear of death? Partially it is because the brain loves predictability. It thrives on routines and habits and a sense of knowing what is ahead. Thoughts of death and even more particularly, thoughts about what happens after death, can cause panic and great fear because the brain cannot predict what these experiences will be like and there is no frame of reference. Thinking about death can cause great distress when it feels like "the end" and the thought that you are just shot out into the abyss after you leave this plane or go to a heaven you don't fully understand can lead to feelings of overwhelm.

But what if you knew that life was eternal?

What if you knew that your life was just one of many your soul would experience and that while you were here on earth, your job was to learn to see the divine already within you, and not only love others, but to see the divine within them as well? What if you knew beyond the shadow of a doubt that death was not the end? How would you choose to live your life then?

I am not a psychic, a medium, or a clairvoyant. I am an ordinary person just like you who has had extraordinary experiences. Ones that have informed me to my very core that death is not the end of our story, but just the next chapter in the evolution of our souls. The stories and experiences I will be sharing with you are my own and those of other people who have experienced things that offer proof that death is not the finality of our soul, but that our soul continues. This is an essential time on our planet to let the light shine on our collective stories of death and beyond so that we can further illuminate the way for others and dispel the grip of death and its finality.

As you read this book you will learn how to calm your fear of death. You will learn how to begin to befriend death as something to be thoughtfully planned for and revered as a sacred next step in your soul's evolution. This is your opportunity to explore your feelings around your life beyond death and listen more deeply to the whisperings of your soul which speak the language of eternity.

We will explore what makes life more precious and meaningful and how you can tap more fully into your eternal essence to enjoy the time you have here on earth and create a more juicy and fulfilling life. Here you will find the tools to navigate life's endings as well. This is a guidebook for your soul. It is a remembrance for your inner being to awaken to the oneness that is this beautiful, and sacred eternal life we all share. It is to remind you that love is still the greatest power of all, both in this life and the next.

At the end of each chapter you will find a "Tapping In" section. A way for you to take the stories and the information in the book and utilize it to grow, expand your self-awareness, heal your relationship with death, and enjoy your life more fully. We are constantly growing and evolving and this is an opportunity to make peace with the inevitable experience of death and embrace the ever-lasting nature of your soul.

This book did not come to you by accident. Something inside of you was ready to have this conversation and perhaps validate a knowingness your soul has been whispering to you for a long time. So, sit down in your favorite chair, grab a cup of tea, take a deep breath (let it go), and let's talk about death and beyond. It's ok. I'm holding your hand as you hold this book. We are in this together.

Chapter One:
The Eternal Spark

"The destination is a happy life, an accomplished life that doesn't end with death but with eternal life."
–ANGELO SCOLA

Since I was a child, my entire life has been built around the idea of a spark, the one essential light that emanates through all of us. Some people call it the soul, or "the God Spark;" the idea that there is something that radiates within us that is eternal. As you begin this journey into the everlasting spark that is you, feel into your heart space and notice the emanating force that is within you. You are not having to make your heart beat, your food digest, or your lungs breathe; something is doing that for you. Something bigger than us, that connects all of us in a beautiful web of existence, is doing all of the work. We just get to come along for the ride. What would happen if you relaxed into the knowingness that the spark that is you will continue on through eternity?

    I have a very clear and vivid memory of exactly where I was when I first thought about life and death. I was five years old in my family's home in the basement standing by my grandmother's antique buffet she had given us that held all of my mom's fine china. I was staring at the multi-colored, short weave carpet we had, nothing special going on at all, when the idea came to me,

"I don't remember being born." I went on to reason in my little head that because I had no memory of being born, I also didn't remember dying before that and so somehow the two must be connected. "We are born and we die and we are born again…we just don't remember."

Strange thoughts for one so young. Perhaps. I feel that I have read and have experienced so many stories coming from the mouths of babes about how they had lived lives before, or at a very young age looked at a picture of a great-grandfather they had never met and exclaimed, "There's Henry! I sure did like him!" Over the course of my career, I have had hundreds of clients in my office who have shared their encounters with loved ones who had passed away and are still in contact with them. Perhaps at five years old I wasn't so far off but had actually discovered my soul's greater truth.

In 1944, Max Planck, the father of quantum theory described a universal field that connects everything in creation; "All matter originates and exists only by virtue of a force…We must assume behind this force the existence of a conscious and intelligent Mind." According to quantum physics, death is not the end. Planck believed in life after death. He believed in the existence of "another world, exalted above ours where we can and will take refuge at any time," and he believed that through prayer and meditation, we could access this world.

In more modern times, in 2014, scientist Robert Lanza made *Time Magazine*'s list of the most 100 influential people in the world. He specializes in stem cells, cloning, and regenerative medicine research. Lanza claims that quantum physics has proven the existence of life after death, that energy is immortal, and so is life. At five years old, I was more interested in baby dolls than the source of the universe, but intuitively I had tapped into a universal truth about our eternal spark that continues on.

When I was six years old my parents hired a housekeeper. Bea would come over on Tuesdays and Thursdays to clean the house, cook meals, and iron my father's shirts. That was the best time for me. While Bea did the ironing, sweat gathering on her forehead, I would sit on the back of the sofa and have long talks with her, about every topic under the sun. I loved her. She was a round woman who would fold me into the warmth of her body when she hugged me and it was a place where I felt safe.

Interestingly, our conversations would often lead to the past lives she had spent taking care of my mother and her brother, my uncle Chuck. She said she had spent lifetimes being their nanny, parent, or teacher. I just listened and took in the stories she shared and never questioned them. Bea wasn't crazy. She was a devout Catholic and a beautiful human being who just shared the facts from her experiences. I grew up thinking conversations and experiences like this were normal, not taboo and to be kept under wraps. My conversations with Bea validated what I knew within my being, that death was not the end of our experience.

In ancient Greece, historical figures, such as Plato and Socrates talked about a belief in the soul's rebirth. Many religions, such as Buddhism, Hinduism, and Jainism, hold reincarnation as a central tenet. Although not all members of these groups believe in reincarnation, they instead believe in an afterlife. The Christian scriptures tell us that we lived before we came to the earth and that because Jesus overcame death, we will continue to live after we die. With so many different reference points leading to the same conclusion, it seems like somebody is on to something here. Our souls go on.

When I am interviewed, I am often asked about my brand, The Spark. My first book is called, "*The Spark-Igniting Your Best Life,*" my first film is, "*When Sparks Ignite,*" and my podcast is called, "*Igniting the Spark.*" What is up with all these sparks? My answer is always the same. I believe that "the spark" is our essence. It's the part of us that is never born and never dies, but just changes shape. The spark is that light that is our soul and although situations or circumstances may seem to dim the shine, it is a light that can never be extinguished, and our work here on earth is to keep excavating that light so we can be clearer conduits for bringing that light into the world.

I remember having this conversation about our sparks with my brother 20 years ago when he converted to Catholicism to marry his wife. I asked him if being Catholic helped him have a deeper understanding of God or our souls. He said it wasn't the church that had enlightened him about this inner truth but that it was the classes he was taking in physics to become an electrical engineer that helped him come to a deeper understanding of it all. He said, "In physics, I learned that matter is never born, and it never dies, it just changes shape." We are that matter, and the energy that is the essential light of God in us that goes on forever. Our essence is that divine spark that continues on long after our body has left this physical plane.

In 2004, the movie, *What the Bleep Do We Know?*, introduced the mainstream to quantum physics and expanded our view of reality. One of the scientists featured in that film is quantum physicist Amit Goswami. In one of my many interviews with him, we explored consciousness, connections, life, death, and the meaning of it all. When I asked Amit, how science validates life after life, he replied, "The empirical data is abundant, it is such a cinch to prove that there is life after life. Our non-local memory can transfer from one life to the next. Our consciousness and our imprinted memory continue in non-local consciousness- meaning it continues on throughout our lifetimes." Non-local consciousness means that our consciousness is not just contained in our body but that we are able to perceive information beyond the reach of our bodies, brains, and senses. Through quantum physics, there is significant proof that our consciousness continues even after our physical body ceases to exist.

CONTINUED ILLUMINATION

My first encounter with death happened when I was thirteen years old. My friend Susan and I had come home from junior high that day and were busy in my room listening to records and gossiping about the boys we liked, and talking about what we were going to wear to the end-of-school dance that Friday. When it was time for Susan to go home, I ran downstairs to the kitchen where my grandma was cooking dinner to ask her if she could give Susan a ride home.

She and my grandfather were living with us during that year because my grandmother had been diagnosed with breast cancer and was receiving chemotherapy and radiation at the hospital that was a block from our home. I had no idea how sick she was. She was the "fun" grandma. Before cancer, she had been the one that would pick my brother and me up from school and take us to 7-11 or McDonald's for a treat once a week. She had a lead foot and a quick wit and was one of those grandmothers who made every grandchild feel like they were her very favorite (and there were 26 of us!)

That afternoon when I went down to the kitchen to ask for my friend's ride, she turned from her cooking and snapped at me. She waved her wooden spoon at me and started yelling at me for asking her to do that. She started cursing at me and began to chase me around the house yielding that wooden spoon like she was going to smack me with it if she caught me. This was totally bizarre behavior for my grandmother. I didn't know what to do. My fight or flight kicked in and when I ran downstairs and she followed, I pushed out the screen from the open window, crawled through, and ran to my next-door neighbors to call my mother. She was still at work at the flower shop she owned and wasn't due home for an hour.

"Mom! Mom! I think Grandma has gone crazy! You've got to come home, now!" I hollered into the phone. I don't remember the rest of the conversation. I only remember that Mom came home right away, Susan came out of my bedroom where she had stayed and locked the door when all the yelling began, and she and my grandfather came out of the house to meet me, so we could take her home.

When we got back, I saw my grandmother, still in the kitchen, stirring something on the stove. Her head hung down and she didn't look up when I walked past. I didn't speak to her. I was still upset from all that had happened. I did realize in that moment that the image of her standing by the stove was the last time I would see my grandmother alive.

I spent the evening in my room and went to bed without talking to anyone else besides my mom about what had happened. "Honey, I think grandma is really sick," she told me. "Well, she doesn't act sick," I replied. It was only later that we found out the cancer had reached her brain and was to blame for her erratic behavior.

That night, I awoke and looked at my clock beside my bed: 3:15 am. I went to the bathroom that was down the hall from my bedroom and on the way back, I heard stirring in my brother's bedroom where my grandparents were sleeping. They had taken it over because it had the bigger bed and my brother slept downstairs in our guest bedroom. Something made me go to the doorway of their room and speak into the darkness, "Grandma, I'm sorry," I whispered loud enough in hopes she would hear it. "It's ok honey," came her soft and warm reply. I crawled into bed and breathed a little bit deeper and felt a little bit lighter. It was all "ok."

The next morning, I was awakened by my mother's screams. I jumped out of bed and ran down the stairs, and there she was, standing with my grandfather. My first thought was, "Oh my god, she's been stabbed!" She was holding her chest and was doubled over, my grandfather holding on to her like he was saving her from drowning in a river. "Mom! What's happening?!" I feared her reply. The words ripped from her mouth in a loud wail, "Grandma's dead!"

"What?!" I couldn't believe this was happening. I ran back up the stairway and into my brother's bedroom where she was still lying; Kleenex in hand, covered by an electric blanket so her body was still warm when I touched her shoulder. Her lightly tinted blue lips were the only hint that gave death away. She looked so peaceful; like she would flutter her eyes open at any moment from her recent slumber, but she was gone.

I remember when the long black car pulled up in our driveway to take her body away to the funeral home. I could see the other children in the neighborhood walking to school and looking at our house to see what all the commotion was. I remember thinking, "Their lives are just the same. Everything outside this window is the same. The world is just going by while our entire lives have changed forever."

At the funeral home, they did a private viewing of her body in the casket before the funeral. It was very clear that the body lying in that box was no longer my grandmother. She looked the same, but the "Her" that I had had endless slumber parties with, made dozens and dozens of chocolate chip cookies with, the grandma that had taught my 4-H cooking group how to decorate cakes, and loved to go fishing, and tell a good joke, that grandma was gone.

It wasn't until twelve years later that I would find out that she had never truly left.

YOUR IMMORTAL SOUL

> "Just living your true being in totality you slowly, slowly become aware of the immortal current of life within you. You know the body will die, but this soul, which is life's whole essence, cannot die."
>
> –OSHO

Although I have shared this story in other places, I felt it was essential to also share in this book, as it is the continuation of my grandmother's story; the awareness that her "ending" wasn't the real end.

At twenty-five years old, I was a single mom putting myself through graduate school. I would drive four days a week from Fort Collins where I lived, to the University of Denver where I would attend nine hours of class each day. My four-year-old daughter Acacia and I lived a very simple life which consisted of a lot of time with my extended family. I remember thanking God that my parents and several aunts and uncles lived in town because not only did I need their emotional support, but I didn't own a computer, and they happily shared theirs which I needed to write my research papers.

After one of those long days of commuting and studying, I was soaking in a bubble bath when the phone rang. These were the days before cell phones, so I had my big porta-phone beside me and quickly picked it up. It was my mother's voice, "Stephanie, I have some bad news for you." I swallowed hard. My aunt Gwen had been diagnosed with breast cancer five years earlier and even after her mastectomy, she was having complications. "What's going on?" I timidly asked, fearing the answer. "When they went in for the exploratory surgery on Gwen this morning, they found that the cancer had spread through her entire body cavity. There was nothing they could do so they sewed her back up and let us know it looks like she only has around three months to live."

I put down the phone and started to cry. That was when little Acacia wandered into the bathroom.

Now, I have to stop for a moment to tell you about Acacia's name. When I was pregnant with her and looking for a name, I had a sense that my baby would be a girl, and when the baby name book I was reading said that "Acacia" was the Greek word for immortality and the tree of life in Africa, I knew that was the one. I had no idea when I chose that name, she would be the one teaching me about the immortality of our souls.

When Acacia walked into the bathroom and saw me upset, she innocently asked me, "Why are you crying, Momma?" "Oh, honey," I responded, "Momma just doesn't want anybody to die." She sat gently on the side of the tub and just looked at me. "But Momma, we never die."

My first thought was that she must be thinking that we go to heaven, although we had never talked about heaven, didn't go to church, and had never even talked about God. She shook her sweet little head at me. "There is no heaven Momma. But when I was a light in the sky with God..." she said, intuitively knowing what we had never spoken of. It was here she stopped and looked at me more closely and then asked, "Do you remember your other mother, Dorothy?" My "other mother, Dorothy." What an interesting phrase. My grandmother Dorothy had been gone for thirteen years and my grandfather had remarried the year after she had passed. The only great-grandma Acacia knew was Grandma Cille, my grandpa's wife. We never had a reason to talk about my grandma Dorothy, nor did I have any pictures of her. But here Acacia was asking me if I remembered my "other mother, Dorothy."

"Well," she continued, "Her light was up in the sky with me and God and God took some of her light and put it with my light and then I got to come down and be your daughter." It gives me chills to this day. Even as I write this. Head to toe. It changed my life. I called my mother back immediately and told her what Acacia had said. We laughed together and cried together and marveled at the reality of what had just unfolded.

It is also interesting to note that as Acacia grew up, her personality was nothing like my grandmother's. I have always had more of my grandmother's personality: never knowing a stranger, outspoken with a big laugh, and very extroverted. Acacia is an artist. She has struggled with social anxiety and has overcome huge obstacles in her life dealing with her introversion. She is an amazingly bright, beautiful, and talented human being, but she was not outwardly like my grandmother. However, when Acacia was about twelve years old, I will always remember my grandfather exclaiming to those of us who sat around the dining room table for dinner that night, "Acacia is the most like Grandma Dorothy out of all of my grandchildren." He had twenty-six. My grandmother was the love of his life, and he sensed her spark inside of Acacia despite what the outside world saw.

You too have this light, this spark inside of you. When you come to understand that this spark will continue on, you will find your ability to savor this beautiful life you have been given more fully, knowing that any difficult circumstance is only temporary, and that death cannot and will not define you because it is not the finality of your journey, only the curtain closing on the play of your life for a brief intermission before your next act.

TAPPING IN:

---

1. Write down your earliest memories of times you had this "knowing" like Acacia. Some wisdom beyond your years or something you experienced as a child that could not be explained by the logical outside world.

2. Take time to review the spiritual experiences you had around death as a child. What messages about death have you carried with you? What has informed your beliefs around death?

3. Breathe into the happiest memory you have of yourself as a child. See yourself playing, laughing, rolling in the grass… doing whatever you most loved to do. That precious child is still alive inside of you. When you are in touch with this part of yourself, you can go beyond social constructs and cultural conditions, to access the eternal element of your soul. This creates a deeper sense of well-being and connectedness to something that goes beyond our daily life experience.

Chapter Two:
Making Peace with It All

> "Whenever death occurs, whenever a life form dissolves, God, the formless and unmanifested, shines through the opening left by the dissolving form. That is why the most sacred thing in life is death. That is why the peace of God can come to you through the contemplation and acceptance of death."
>
> —ECKHART TOLLE

What does it mean to make peace with death? Does it mean you welcome its arrival, look forward to it as a new adventure, and befriend it as being a part of the natural life-death-life cycle? Well, in a word, "Yes." Let me explain. What it means is that you are able to live this life as fully and as beautifully as possible and let go of dreading the end, because it is not the end. To make peace with death is to accept that death is a part of life and just a transition to another state of beingness that you have not yet experienced. You can savor every moment of this amazing life you have been given and let go of the fear of the finality of death and the anxious pressure of the ticking clock telling you that you are running out of time.

In the words of Henry David Thoreau in *Walden*, "*I went to the woods because I wished to live deliberately, to front only the essential facts of life, and see if I could not learn what it had to teach, and not, when I came to die, discover that I had not lived. I did not wish to live what was not life, living is so dear; nor did I wish to practice resignation, unless it was quite necessary. I wanted to live deep and suck out all the marrow of life ...."*

What would your life look like if you "sucked out all the marrow?" Would you spend endless hours in front of your computer or TV screen, worrying about things that are out of your control, engaging in petty arguments with those you work with or love, or would you walk in nature, dance in the rain, hug your loved ones closer, or sing out loud in the shower? It is a powerful process to pause and take inventory of the people, activities, and things in your life that are meaningful to you; the ones that light up your soul, and then choose to focus on how you can better connect with those things that bring you joy. When you let go of your fear of death you can plug into how to be more fully alive. Knowing that death is just a transitory state into a new state of being, can give you the freedom to explore this life more fully, love more deeply, and shine more brightly because there is no fear of your soul's experience coming to an abrupt ending. Yes, on this 3D plane your physical form will cease to exist. However, while life on this earth for you will end, your soul will continue, experiencing its own adventures.

THE PEACE PROCESS

Part of making peace with death has to do with making peace with life first. Instead of pushing death away, as we make peace with the process, the reality of death can actually become the foundation and the springboard that allows us to live our lives more intentionally. So often I have clients in my office who share stories of shame and regret, and things they wish they would have said to loved ones who have passed. Their lives have become unmanageable emotionally because the past is taking up so much room in the present. Once they begin the process of bringing compassion to themselves and their loved one, and truly letting go of the past, they are able to heal into the present and then begin to create what I call, "A life by design," where they are no longer the victims of life but rather, co-creators with it. What would happen if you let go of your story; if you no longer allowed it to define you or take up space in the present moment?

We all have a natural negativity bias in our brains that focuses on potential threats "out there," which includes our fear of death, so it can kick into a fight, flight, or freeze mode to try and save our lives (even if we don't need saving.) This happens instantaneously and our bodies are flooded with cortisol and adrenaline so we can run or fight our way to survival. We are hardwired this way. We can fixate on the fragility of life, as our brains keep returning to our fear of death, because it is our most primal instinct to survive. However, the good news is we can do something about it to change our brain's natural conditioning. By cultivating the simple practices of meditation, breathwork, and present-moment awareness, we can keep leading our brains into a relationship with what is here and now instead of ruminating about the past or worrying about the future (which includes our fear of death.) Through practice and repetition, we can begin carving new neural pathways that cultivate a sense of wellbeing and peace within us.

Our brain loves predictability, and sudden changes in our lives, or the death of a loved one can also put our brain into fight, flight, or freeze mode because there is often no frame of reference for what is happening. We are convinced that we have some sort of control in our lives through calendars and planning and setting goals for ourselves. As difficult as it may be to wrap our heads around, we are not in control of much of anything. Yes, we can make decisions and act in the moment, but our ability to control things around us, what will happen later today, tomorrow, or next year, are illusions.

I am not saying that you can just flip a switch and then, "Voilà!" all the past is healed and forgiven, and never again will you have an anxious thought about death or the future. What I am saying is that through daily practice of going within and being in touch with the Divine within you (no matter what is happening in that moment), you will begin to notice an ease and grace that permeate your experience of it all. How do you get in touch with that Divine within? It is as accessible as pausing right now and bringing all of your attention to your heart center and breathing into it. Put your hand on your heart and feel into your chest. Who is beating that heart for you?

What also can help you let go of the fear of death is remembering what many masters have told us, "The kingdom of God is within." In Luke 17:20-21, Jesus, being asked by the Pharisees when the kingdom of God would come, answered them, "The kingdom of God is not coming in ways that can be observed, nor will they say, 'Look, here it is!' or 'There!' for behold, the kingdom of God is within you." You are not separate from God in life and you most certainly won't be separate from God after death, because God, who is also a part of your divine essence, is always within you.

Oftentimes, people are very afraid of death because they are afraid they won't make it into heaven. Beloved Zen Master Thich Nhat Hanh, global spiritual leader, poet, and peace activist, revered around the world for his pioneering teachings on mindfulness, said in *his Dharma Talk: The Keys to the Kingdom of God,*

"I said that the Kingdom of God is right now, right here, and you don't have to die to step into the Kingdom of God. In fact, you have to be very alive in order to step into it. For me being alive is to be mindful, to be concentrated, to be free. That is the kind of passport you need to be allowed into the Kingdom of God: mindfulness, concentration, freedom." You don't have to earn anything to get into heaven, heaven is already within you. There are specific practices from breathwork, to meditation, to ecstatic prayer that can allow you to access that heaven now.

In my life I have thought many times that perhaps heaven or hell were not places we go to when we die, but what we experience between our ears. When we are caught in negativity and worries, we experience a kind of internal hell and when we can surrender to what is happening in the present moment and drop out of our heads and into our hearts, we are able to experience a state of heaven or bliss.

However you may think of this "Kingdom Within" from your particular background or spiritual orientation, is absolutely fine. It is the concept of heaven and hell I am looking at here; the archetype or the metaphor of it, not defined locations to debate. There is power in cultivating this heavenly state inside of you. When you sit in the present moment and let go of anything having to be other than what it is, you will begin to be at peace. Death then is not something to be feared because you are living in the kingdom of your life and can continue cultivating peace until your last breath. If you allow yourself to marinate on the phrase, "As above, so below," you can begin to see how cultivating a peaceful life that feels like heaven on earth, will deeply serve you. You can create this sense of heaven within you. It is something you keep cultivating throughout your lifetime.

PRACTICING PEACE

When we cling to our life or death having to be a certain way, we suffer. I am reminded of when I took my oldest daughter to her last treatment center over seven years ago. We had been struggling with her drug and alcohol addiction for a decade. A straight 'A' student through her entire academic career, a star soccer player, and the lead of the school play her senior year; she had instantly become addicted to oxycodone when she was offered it by her boyfriend in those first months after she left for college. Some of the most difficult moments of my entire life and my family's lives were during those years. But no time was as challenging as those last three months when she was in treatment and my three and four year old grandsons lived with me.

Married to a multi-millionaire, I was living a very carefree life. Traveling around the globe, living in a big, beautiful house with all the luxuries I could have ever wanted or imagined. And then, suddenly I was alone with the boys.

For the first week they were at my home, my husband was on a business trip, and I was working full-time in my private practice, while trying to handle two precious, wounded, and scared little boys. There was one night when I was literally on my knees, sobbing and asking God, "Why?! Why is this happening to me?!!" I was so angry at God, at my daughter, and at this new situation that had robbed me of any freedom and left me emotionally and physically exhausted. My marriage had begun to suffer and would eventually end due to his lack of support for my daughter and grandsons. I had to deal with the pressure of all that was happening in my life alone.

I said out loud to God, "I didn't choose this life!" And then, while still on my knees, something came over me. I felt a warmth and Divine presence around and within me. I suddenly realized that I was the one creating more of my own pain and suffering. By resisting what was happening and being angry about it, I was creating my own hell of overwhelm, resentment, and anger. At that moment, in the depths of my heart, I surrendered everything in my life over to the Divine. I surrendered the outcome of my daughter's treatment, the daily challenges I was experiencing, the crumbling of my marriage, and the need to control anything that was happening around me. I knew there was nothing I could do to change anything. I became profoundly aware there was nothing to be *done* at all; just surrender.

I slept peacefully that night for the first time in months and that peace continued. My beautiful daughter came back from that treatment center and after surrendering to her own sense of a higher power and doing the incredible, profound work of personal healing, she has remained clean and sober for over seven years. It has been one of the biggest gifts in my life.

I use this example because at one point I was so painfully holding onto the life I had, I was creating suffering in my experience of trying to control everything that was happening. When we cling to past chapters of our lives, we are not allowing the beauty of the next chapter of our life to be written. When we hold onto life having to look a certain way and death having to come in a certain way for us to be happy or at peace, we are creating our own misery. The way through the multiple chapters of our lives, is to meet each part with dignity, grace, and acceptance of what is, so when we reach our final chapter, death becomes only the temporary ending that informs us, "Yes, there is indeed a sequel."

LETTING GO

When you lose a loved one, there can be a part of you that is angry at God or life. You don't understand how your loved one could have been taken away from you. Just as I was angry that my easy, jet-set life was taken away from me and nothing was the same anymore. There are events like death or loss in your life that can feel like there was your "before the event" life and your "after the event" life where everything feels like it has changed. And it has. What makes us so resistant to change?

We can predict what might happen during our days. We have schedules that dictate to us what is going to "happen" hour by hour, but the reality is that we really don't know. And, it's ok that we don't know. I deeply believe in the power of goal setting, visualization, and the power of our thoughts to create the lives we want. And when we let go of the false sense of control that things have to happen when and how we want them to, we can relax into our lives in a new way. We can make peace with the present moment. It doesn't *have* to *be* anyway. We can accept what is here now and move into a point of peace and power in just being with our experience exactly as it is.

Practicing present moment awareness when things are painful can be difficult. You might want to numb out or distract yourself or push down your feelings. The thing about that is when we reject our feelings they just lie in wait to come out later with more vengeance. One strategy of befriending the present moment is to just breathe deeply into your body repeating "I breathe in love, I breathe out pain, I rest in the now." This can help you move stuck energy that is resisting what is happening when painful events occur.

In the famous words of Neale Donald Walsch, "What you

resist, persists." When you are in a stage of anger and resistance to the circumstances in your life, you create suffering. As you move into acceptance, you move into peace. I am reminded of a story where a man experiences both good and bad events in his life. As each one happens, he responds with, "And this." as a way of holding both the positive and the negative events in the same energy, knowing that experiences, people, and emotions come and go. Michael Singer in his book, "Living Untethered" says that, "Suffering is when we want this moment to be anything other than what it is." Making peace with the present moment is a practice. It's like building a muscle that through repetition, you are able to relax into and utilize as it becomes more and more a continual state of being.

BEFRIENDING YOUR FEAR

I understand how the concept of befriending death might sound absurd, but what if you just befriended your fear of death first? In my therapy office, I often tell clients about the need to just accept and befriend whatever emotion is showing up inside of them, and that our angst is increased when we get angry that we are angry, feel sad that we are sad, and anxious that we might get anxious. The same is true when you focus on your fear of death. It can feel overwhelming, and the fear can get amplified. In dealing with the different emotions that can show up inside of us, the great 13th-century Sufi poet Rumi, in his poem *"The Guest House,"* tells us to meet these emotions at the door of our lives laughing and invite them in because "…each has been sent as a guide from beyond."

You can start this process of befriending your fear by first acknowledging when it shows up. We live in a world full of distractions. Your phone, computer, and social media, among other things, are all vying for your attention. You may drink, shop, or numb out on video games as a way to not feel your feelings. But when you do that, I promise, they are waiting for you and then they will return with more intensity. The late, great Wayne Dyer used to say that when we keep those feelings inside of us, we are creating dis-ease or disease within us.

Start by just allowing the fear to be there and notice where it shows up in your body. Instead of connecting the feeling to "a story" you may have about it, just notice how the fear feels within you. Is it tight? Is it heavy or dense? You may even notice if it feels like it has a texture, a temperature, or a color. Naming your emotions can help tame your emotions. It gives the emotion a degree of separation from you. "I am *feeling* scared," has a very different meaning than, "I *am* scared." You are not your feelings; you are the one experiencing them.

Once you are in touch with the feeling in your body, just breathe into it. You may even imagine a Divine light coming in through the top of your head and start directing it into the space where you are experiencing the fear. Allow it to penetrate and permeate each and every particle of your fear. Allow that light to go in, around, and through the emotion and notice what happens. When I do this exercise with clients in my office, they often report a feeling of lightness and that what was once "a tight ball of fear" begins to dissipate and disappear.

Another powerful exercise, that I learned from my co-leader, Phoebe Leona on my most recent women's retreat I led in Mexico, was the process of writing a letter directly to your emotions. So again, when that fear comes up, notice where it is in your body, so you get a sense of where it is living in you at the moment. Then pull out a notebook or journal and write a letter directly to that fear. Don't edit your thoughts or other feelings around the fear, just let the words flow onto the paper.

To begin with, it might look something like, "I HATE YOU FEAR! You make me feel like I can't breathe, and you take away my joy and you rob me of living my life in the way I want to. GO AWAY!!!" Just allow yourself to keep writing and writing until it feels like all of your words are out. This may just be a few paragraphs, or it might be pages and pages. However long the letter turns out to be is irrelevant. What is important is that you express yourself fully to this feeling.

And now for the truly powerful part. Once you are done with the letter, pause, take a couple of nice deep belly breaths, and then have your fear write a letter back to you. Yes, you read that right. Have your fear take on its own voice and just intuitively write a letter back to yourself and see what it has to say to you.

I was personally blown away by this process. When I wrote a letter to my fear, it said back to me, "*Stephanie, I had no idea that I was causing this angst in your body. I have only shown up to protect you and keep you safe. I felt like I had to yell so loudly so you would not be harmed by other people. I can see now that I didn't trust you and your beautiful heart to know the best way for you to go through life. I thought I had to rescue you. I can see now, I do not. I promise I will quiet down and truly try to just be here when you really need me. If I forget and show up unannounced, just remind me that you've got this, and I will calm down and back off immediately. I love you. Sincerely, Fear.*"

Transformational, indeed. And, if you want to start with an emotion different from fear to begin with, practice first by just writing a letter to an emotion that is easier for you to feel. Write a letter to your joy and have it write you back and see what the process feels like. Practice looking into your feelings from their vantage point. As you begin to feel more comfortable with the process, you can allow yourself to move into your more challenging feelings with more ease.

BEFRIENDING DEATH

The Tibetan Book of the Dead is a guidebook for the living, although originally, it was read aloud by a Tibetan Buddhist monk to let a newly departed soul know what it was encountering so that the transition would be more peaceful as it moved through this intermediate state to a new form of being. Its text teaches one how to approach death with preparation and offers comfort in the promise of continued existence. Currently, hospice workers often use this text to calm the fears of the dying to help them let go of their present life and embrace a new experience with an understanding that their soul will go on after death.

My aunt Gwen was reading this book while she was dying. I remember seeing it on her coffee table the night I went over to help shave her head when her hair had begun to fall out from all of the radiation and chemotherapy. That night was such a powerful experience for me because instead of it being sorrowful and somehow traumatic, my aunt asked me to put on her favorite Mozart music, and with it streaming through the living room walls, we shared stories of our peak experiences in life as the whir of the clippers erased the clumps of hair she had left. It was beautiful. Stunning in its soulfulness. She knew she was dying and instead of making the experience of losing her hair something tragic, she used it as a way for us to celebrate the magical moments of being fully alive.

A few weeks later, I met her for coffee at one of our favorite local cafes. She was wearing a colorful scarf and these large, gold hoop earrings and I remember thinking how cool she looked, like some exotic gypsy. I don't remember much of our conversation. However, I know at some point, as I looked into her smiling eyes and we laughed together at something one of us had just said, it struck me to my core: This beautiful woman in front of me, my aunt I adored, so seemingly full of life in the moment, in a very short time was no longer going to be here. I reached across the table and grabbed both of her arms in mine, and with large tears streaming down my face cried, "Why is this happening?! Do you really want to die?!" I truly believed at that time, that somehow inside of us, we made either a conscious or unconscious decision to leave the planet and that we had more control over that decision than for death to just happen to us without our consent.

"Of course, I don't want to die," she said softly, "I want to live. And I have to accept that my death will just be a part of my living. I will just continue in a different form." Those words fell gently on my aching heart. We cried together and continued to hold arms. I didn't want to let go. Even though she didn't want to die, she was moving into this dance with death, knowing it would be her next partner to waltz her into the mystery of what was beyond this life. I breathed big gulps of acceptance out of the air and with her, began to make peace with the process she had entered.

A few months later, when the cancer had spread unbelievably fast through her body, her personality faded, and her body began to shut down. At only forty-six years old, it felt so bizarre that she would need to be put into a nursing home, so she could receive around-the-clock care. She couldn't speak anymore or feed herself. Her body was so full of fluid that her skin had started cracking and weeping. She didn't recognize us when we came into the room to visit. It felt as if her body was still there, but her spirit had already exited.

Until one day in early October, the last day I ever saw her, I got the idea that she needed to go outside. My aunt Gwen had always loved the changing color of the leaves and that fall, the trees were on fire with vibrant yellows and oranges and reds. I felt like regardless of whether her personality was gone, her body would enjoy the warmth of the sun. The nurses told me she wasn't in any physical pain due to all the medication she was on and that it would be ok for me to take her out into the front yard of the nursing home if I stayed on the sidewalk. They lovingly helped me get her into a wheelchair and cover her with a blanket.

I wheeled my aunt out of those doors that felt like they were holding their breath and into the brilliant sunshine and thick aroma of fall that settled in all around us. She sat still in her trancelike state. I secured the brake on the wheelchair and then knelt before her, looking into her glassy eyes, and then it happened. Something… some spark, some spirit blinked into her eyes and a sweet smile brushed her lips. Connection! Her soul had inhabited her body and for that brief moment, she was fully there. And then as quickly as it had appeared, it faded back into the blankets on her lap, and the stare into nothingness returned. But I had seen her. The light that was her, shining triumphantly from beyond.

US OR THEM

> "Death is not life's cul-de-sac. It is an extension of that road once traveled. Though you must go one way and I another, we can and will reunite and resume our journey together."
>
> −STEWART STAFFORD

When you think about the fear of death, I would also ask you another question, "How much of it is the fear of losing someone you love?" In my life, I have been at peace with the fact that the life that I am experiencing through this body and personality I call, "Stephanie," will one day cease to exist on this plane. I don't plan on or want to die for a long time because I want to be here to experience my children, family, grandchildren, dear friends, and this amazing world for as long as I possibly can. I LOVE life. I am thoroughly enjoying the ride *and* I also know that one day, my ride on this particular merry-go-round will be over.

What can still sneak up and bring tears to my eyes in an instant, is the thought of losing my 80-year-old mother and stepfather. They have been my rock and my source of unconditional love during my life; people who believed in me and saw my potential when I could not find the greatness in me. They have held me through the worst of times, celebrated my accomplishments, and have been my biggest cheerleaders through it all. I cannot imagine a world where these two do not exist. Every holiday with my mother is something special. There is always room for one more at their table, the house is always decorated for all occasions, and my mother's thoughtfulness makes sure everyone feels included. They are the hub in the wheel of our family.

There are moments when fear creeps in and I think, "No one can ever love me as much as my mom." I wonder, "How will I survive when she is gone?" At times, I am comforted by remembering that she will never truly be "gone." Her love and her legacy will live on inside of me and inside of my children and theirs and I know that her soul will continue even after she is physically gone. Her light that has illuminated all our lives will go on forever. What comforts me and relieves this fear is when I remember the countless stories from clients, friends, family, and others who have experienced a loved one returning in some way after they have passed. I have also had several of my own experiences that have informed me, without a doubt, that there is a Divine presence that we are all a part of and it is alive in us. The essence of who we are, our spirit or soul, will continue.

So how can you let go of the fear of losing those you love on the physical plane and make peace with this particular fear? I believe one of the most powerful things you can do to start with, is to drop out of your head and into your heart to feel the connection you have with this other person. Even if that person isn't with you at the moment, you can feel the essence of who they are and your connection with them. Marinate on that good feeling and let it spread through your being. You might remember a special time with them or imagine them smiling and tap into the feeling of joy and love between you. As you do this practice, you will begin to experience more peace within you and a greater sense of wellbeing. Your connections with your loved ones are timeless. They are live experiences happening within you in the present moment.

It is powerful because our minds believe that whatever is held in attention is happening now. That is why you can look back to a painful memory and feel regret or guilt. The situation isn't happening in the present moment, but your mind perceives it as happening "now" and releases the hormones and chemicals that equal the feelings of regret or guilt in your body. The same is true if you play the "What If" game with the future and start to feel anxious or afraid. The future isn't happening now, but as your mind holds up the negative scenarios of what *could* happen, your physiological response to those thoughts is as if the negative is already happening. When you practice focusing on the connection you feel to others you love in your heart instead, you will train your mind to focus on creating positive feelings in the now of your life.

Although it may feel counterintuitive, another strategy is to acknowledge to yourself the truth that your loved ones' days here on earth, in physical form are finite but your ability to connect with them is infinite. You can use that information to step into the power of the present moment and move into action. What do you want to say to or do with one of your loved ones while they are still here on earth? Think about the things that you may have wanted to tell someone you love and then go do it! Researcher Martin Seligman, in his research at Pennsylvania State University, concludes, that if you want a substantial "joy boost" in your life, don't just write a letter to a loved one and send it in the mail, go read it to them in person (if you are able) and see how it lands in their heart. It is a joy boost for both them and you. (Zoom also works great for this too!)

When I catch myself in those moments of fear or sadness thinking about the potential loss of my parents, I drop out of my head and fearful thoughts, breathe into my heart, and then move into action. I call my mother, I walk down to their house for a cup of coffee (I am blessed that they live only six blocks away.) I invite them out for dinner or ask how we can best connect, and I let them know they matter. I say, "I love you," as often as possible. In my family, when my daughter Acacia was a little girl, my stepfather started saying to her, "I love you a million apple pies!" and a huge smile would come across her face as she said those same words right back to him. How better to express a love so huge? There is not a week that goes by that I don't say that out loud to one of my parents. I write it on the bottom of birthday cards or just send it as a quick text as a way to express my love for them which is immeasurable.

Don't wait. I can't tell you how many clients I have had in my office who have held deep regrets for not picking up the phone, making the trip, or having that extra dinner with a loved one before they passed unexpectedly. Again, it is not to do these things out of fear. Move into your heart and hold the image of your loved one and see them smiling. Feel your heart and energy connecting with them and imagine them in a state of joy. Now, from this place, you can move into action with love. When you befriend death, you are aware that it will visit you and your loved ones at some point, but the essential piece is that you have the power to decide how and where you are going to spend your precious time while you are living.

What if by befriending death, you allowed yourself to show up as the very best version of yourself? As you become more thoughtful around death, you become more thoughtful about your life. It's not about outrunning death, it is about embracing its inevitability and moving into a life full of meaning. It's about what is important to you in this life, not just off the top of your head, but down in the crevasses of your heart. When you acknowledge that your time and the time of your loved ones is limited on this plane (although the connection will continue) you begin to let go of the fear that binds you and you begin to step into the love that is never-ending.

NEXT STEPS

When you allow yourself to think about death, yours and the deaths of others, it is not a curse or somehow magically going to cause you or your loved ones to die. We are so afraid of death as a culture, we don't allow ourselves to think about and explore death until often it is literally too late and our loved one has suddenly passed and it feels as if the world has exploded. Of course it is painful to lose anyone you love but you can ease that pain when you become aware that death is merely a bridge to the next expression of life. Having conversations about death and exploring its mysteries will actually bring you more peace. It's okay to feel sad and scared. Allow yourself those feelings and journal, write, draw, or paint your way to making more peace with them.

Writing about what you would like to have happen at your funeral or celebration of life is a powerful exercise. Talking about the legacy you want to leave when you pass can help motivate you to make important changes or take action in the present. Discussing how you might feel or what you might do when a loved one passes may actually give you inspiration to write that heartfelt letter, make time to be with those you love, or speak the words that your heart has been longing to say. It is when you lean into what at first might feel uncomfortable that it becomes easier to bear.

When I worked at an elementary school for ten years, I taught character building classes in all of the classrooms. One of the strategies for kids who were afraid of monsters or things they considered scary was to have them draw the monster in as much detail as possible. Afterwards, they would describe their monster or scary thing that they had drawn and then they could rip up the picture, stomp on it, or crumple it up as a way of feeling empowered and letting go of their fears. It wasn't by ignoring it. It was by making the monster even more real, discussing it and then feeling those feelings that allowed them to create mastery over it. When you explore your thoughts and feelings about death you are creating your own mastery over that fear.

I was at a dear friend's for dinner when he brought up the concept of "Death Dinners." He told me he had been reading about how these dinners had become more popular as a way to bring something out into the light that has been held in conversational darkness. It is when a group of people get together and have a wonderful meal in a beautiful setting and the topic of the evening is death. It is a way for people to expel their fears, find common threads, and explore this mysterious realm together, bringing light to the topic and more wellbeing to their souls.

When you share your experiences of death, you can experience oneness with other people in your shared experiences. You are not alone. As you go deeper with others and allow yourself to discuss death you will find your life takes on deeper meaning, becomes more precious, and you will begin to see the sacred and interconnectedness in all of life. Bodies may die but it is not the end. The consciousness that is your essence and your connection to all that is, continues. That sense of oneness or connection to the eternal is not a single experience that just sages and holy men get to experience. It is yours to experience, right now, in this moment. It's as close as your heartbeat. There is nothing to believe or even think about. It is the timelessness of this moment, pregnant with possibilities, as you breathe it in and just listen.

In my film, *When Sparks Ignite*, Dr. Larry Dossey spoke about this oneness and the essential message, that based on solid science we now know that consciousness is not just contained within the body; it always has been and always will be independent of the body. It is eternal and immortal. Together our collective consciousness creates what Larry refers to as the "one mind." This is our eternal interconnectedness and the emanating light that continues on after we have left this physical reality. How might you begin to befriend death if you discussed it from this framework of eternity? When you embrace this everlasting connection with all of consciousness, you realize that you can never lose anyone because you *are* one with that light that exists within and through us all.

Larry finished his on-stage presentation with a beautiful quote from the 13th-century Persian poet Hafiz, that speaks to our eternal connection with each other that is perfect here. *"Let's go deeper, go deeper. For if we do, our spirits will embrace and interweave, and our union will be so glorious that even God will not be able to tell us apart."*

TAPPING IN:

---

1. You are hardwired with the fight-or-flight response, so it is normal to have fearful responses to things that are unknown. At this moment (yes, I mean, right now) take a deep breath and then cross your arms in front of you with your opposite hand resting on your opposite shoulder. Begin to lightly tap each shoulder individually, alternating taps. Repeat the words, "All is well, all is well, and all will be well," and notice how your entire being begins to relax. You can utilize this technique at any moment the fear starts to arise and it will engage your parasympathetic nervous system and you will begin to feel the calm spread through you.

2. Knowing that just because you have a thought doesn't make it true, what false beliefs around death and dying are no longer serving you? Write these down in one column on a page and then in the second, write the belief that would serve your heart and soul better. An example of this might be something like: "False belief: Death is going to be painful. New Belief: I lovingly experience life and death as peaceful continuations of the One Life." See if there is a belief in the second column that really lights up your spirit and begin to say it as an affirmative mantra during the day. Hold the feeling of that new belief in your heart as you say it. Feel what it feels like to believe it is true. After continued repetition, the new belief will begin to take root and the old one will begin to wither and fade away.

3. Think about who you might talk with to further explore your feelings about death. Is there a friend? A support group in your town or online? Allow yourself to find the resources to discuss death in a way that begins to dismantle the silent shroud held around it. When we name something we tame it. Talk about your thoughts, feelings and experiences with death and open up the conversation of the timeless. The person sitting beside you on the bus, working beside you in the next cubicle, or standing beside you in the grocery line may have the same questions and curiosities. Together you can dispel the darkness around death and through your open hearted discussions, bring new information to light.

Chapter Three:
The Divine Within

> "I looked in temples, churches and mosques,
> but I found the Divine within my heart."
> –RUMI

If you are looking for the big "T" truth for answers about life and death and what comes after, the answers may not be outside of you, but gathered in the corners and creases of your heart. When you slow down and make an effort to connect to the eternal and divine wisdom that resides inside of you, you will find the answers you are looking for. When you get caught in thoughts, theories, or conditioned thinking, you are resisting going beyond basic thought forms to arrive at a greater truth. In thinking about how important it is that we realize that all of our thoughts aren't true, I go to the great psychiatrist David Burns who is one of the fathers of Cognitive/Behavioral therapy and the author of Feeling Good which has sold over four million copies. It is important to note three things he describes that are the basis of Cognitive/Behavioral therapy. They are:

1. All our emotions are generated by our 'cognitions' – thoughts. How you feel at any given moment is due to what you are thinking about.

2. Depression is the constant thinking of negative thoughts.

3. The majority of negative thoughts that cause us emotional turmoil are usually plain wrong or at least distortions of the truth, but we accept them without question.

I bring this up because it is essential for us to know that just because we think something doesn't make it the big "T" Truth. Our thoughts and fears about death are just that. Thoughts. When something beyond our thoughts connects with our being we know it because it resonates within us. Something in us radiates a warmth when we are in the presence of a greater truth than conditioned cognitions. I call how this registers in my body, my truth bumps. They are my body's signal to me instantaneously that I have just heard or witnessed something that resonates with a higher truth beyond my thoughts. As you move beyond your negative thoughts about death you will be able to recognize this within your own being and will know it by the deep calm peace that resonates in your soul.

At the end of his life, Albert Einstein concluded that our normal, hamster-wheel experience of life is an illusion. While we are on that hamster-wheel, our thoughts, energy, and lives just go round and round while, underneath the surface of it all, time is this whole other dimension where the past and the present and the future merge and become, what Einstein referred to as, "deep time," where there's nowhere to get to and nowhere to go. So what would happen if you chose to step off of the wheel and allowed yourself to move into your timeless essence instead? What if, like in the *Wizard of Oz*, you allowed yourself to look behind the curtain of your life, and found out that the frantic person behind the controls was actually just your mind perpetuating the whole grand illusion?

CHAPTER THREE: THE DIVINE WITHIN

ALL ONE

In my early 30s I had a profound experience of meeting my first holy man. I was attending a Sufi school in San Francisco for a week training on how to become a clearer conduit for helping others to heal. There were lectures, meditations, and practice sessions where each one of us would pair up with another person and practice bringing in Divine light more fully to our hearts and sharing that healing energy with the other. It was a powerful and beautiful practice. Towards the last couple of days of the week, the teachers shared with us that Sidi, a holy man who was the keeper at the Mount of Olives in Jerusalem, was in America and was visiting his son who lived right outside of San Francisco in Marin County. They said they didn't know if he would be making an appearance at the school or not, but wanted to share with us what an incredible man and Divine conduit he was and that there was a possibility of his appearance.

 I had heard of Sidi before. My father and stepmother had attended the school years before, which is how I had found out about it in the first place. They had shared about the nights of meditation and praying, and how Sidi would lead these amazing sessions sometimes running around the room in ecstasy into the wee hours of the morning. In his 70s, my parents said Sidi had more energy than them all. I knew he was a profound healer and that he communed with the Divine beyond what I had experienced. I was so excited at the potential of meeting him. But in the end, he never came to the school that week.

 Walking out of the building on that last day of classes, I approached one of the teachers, Norine. She had known my parents and she and I had connected during the week discussing them. She asked me how I felt about the week and all we had experienced. "My heart is so open and expansive," I told her. "I feel a profound shift within me and a knowingness that this is only the beginning." She smiled at me and I felt the warmth of her loving heart shining through her eyes.

"The only thing," I said, "is that I wish I would have gotten to meet Sidi. I have heard *so* much about him!" I felt a little ache in my heart thinking I had missed him. "Well, we are about to go over to his son's home and see him right now," she replied, "I will call him and ask him if you can come with us. He is very connected and very direct, so if he doesn't feel it is right, he will just say, "No," so be prepared." I felt a wave of energy surge through me. Just the possibility of meeting him was so exciting to me. "Ok! Whatever he says is ok with me," I said, "I'm just happy that you are even asking him if I can go with you."

I remember feeling the minutes as they ticked by while Norine went around the car to call him in private. I remember feeling the sun on my bare arms and how it was sinking into my flesh like a warm healing balm while I waited. Norine walked back around the side of the car and as she approached me, she held out her arms wide and exclaimed, "He said, "Welcome."

The drive over the Golden Gate bridge on the way to Sidi's son's home, felt like the passageway to a mystical place on the other side. As we drove into the forest, towards his son's home, the trees, flowers, and plants all seemed to be illuminated. Time felt like it was taking on a different meaning, as if it was holding its breath and us within it, in a sense of timelessness.

I don't remember the house or walking in from the car. What is clear is sitting on a wooden floor among a dozen others who had come to hear Sidi speak. Sidi sat on the couch in front of us and the room got very still.

He spoke for close to an hour. In his broken English, the

heart of his message was, "We are all one." He told us, "There are no Catholics, no Jews, no Christians, no Muslims, no man, no woman, no black, no white, no death…it is all one." The words sunk into my being and extended through my consciousness to take on far more meaning than just the words themselves. The reality of those words held a sacredness, a knowingness that went far beyond cultural or religious conditioning. It was in the fibers of my being that I recognized this inner truth. It vibrated through my cells, awakening all that was held within me and ignited the spark in my spirit that knew the timeless truth of those words. Beyond our thoughts, emotions, and personalities the Divine within us connects us to one another and to life eternal because we all share a spark from one ultimate Divine source. Like billions of water drops in the ocean of eternity, we are all one.

When you separate yourself from others because of perceived differences, you cultivate a sense of being alone and isolated. When you feel into your interconnectedness and interdependence with all of life, something in you begins to awaken. When you get to the base of human experience you realize that we all have a shared humanity that is inseparable from you because each person, including you, is an important and intricate part of the whole web. Every human being feels pain, experiences moments of joy, goes through profound grief, and has moments of hope. Every human being will experience loss and the death of their loved ones and eventually will die themselves. You will die too. You can begin to live now in a way that expresses the fullness of your heart and allows you to feel this Divine connection to your highest self, and the whole of life and our shared experiences. Knowing that your eternal spark continues, is an entry point for awareness. Knowing that *that* spark is in every sentient being gives immeasurable value to each and every life on the planet.

Religion can be a beautiful gateway to the divine. Where it does not serve is when religious dogma creates separation and puts people into the "good people" (Us) vs. the "bad people" (Them) categories. It creates a harmful narrative that you are only going to heaven (and sometimes only worthy of living) if you believe what "We" believe. We have to go beyond the constructs and confines of religion to the true source of the Divine within each one of us. It is what the mystics in many religions practiced. They went beyond the dogma to the essential message that is the oneness of us all; that God is love, that we are love, and that we are all on the same playing field, each one of us an essential element in the cosmic body of the universe. How is this interpretation missed? Power, control, and the political and social agendas of some groups of people, have tried to keep us in the delusion that we are separate. If we keep returning to the Divine spark within us, it is all love. It is a place of total oneness with all that is. If there is no separation, how can we hate someone who is different from us? They *are* us.

In my film, *When Sparks Ignite*, Larry Dossey also shares the research correlating spirituality and medicine that has exploded in American medical education. Larry said, "We know based on about 40 years of collected data, that those people who follow some sort of spiritual path in their life, it doesn't seem to matter which one they choose, (which causes some people a lot of indigestion), on average they live seven to thirteen years longer than people who do not." He shared that spirituality is that sense of connectedness with something higher than the individual self or ego. "It's a felt connection with an absolute and imminent or transcendent power, whatever name you want to apply to that. It applies a conviction to meaning and value and direction and purpose as valid aspects of this world we live in."

What happens when you focus on the meaning, value, and joint purpose in life and death instead of whose definition of how to get to heaven is right or wrong? What would happen if you stopped defining yourself by religion, race, or belief systems and instead went beyond dogma and differences to where you can truly see and hold others in compassion and kindness in the interiors of your heart. What would this world look like if you held life and death in this sacred framework of shared experience? I would invite you to do your own internal inventory. See how different it feels when you move into the contents of your soul and connect with that eternal shared spark that is in you, and in me, and in the person standing beside you in the checkout line. What would happen if you just looked for the diamond sparkling heart and eternal light in others? You would see the everlasting light that goes beyond time, space, and circumstance that intricately connects us all unending.

The peak moments in my life have been those where I am experiencing this sense of oneness and connection to the sacred. It is a sense of the eternal, the preciousness of the soul, and a knowingness that we are all deeply connected to all of life. It is these soul connections that inform me that we are beyond the flesh and bones of our bodies and so much more than what we "see" on the exterior plane of life. The healing of ourselves and our planet depends on us being in touch with this connection we have to all sentient beings. This connection was beautifully stated by the beloved yogi, Maharishi Mahesh, the creator of Transcendental Meditation, when he was asked, "How should we treat others?" the yogi replied, "There are no others."

THE GIFT OF FLIGHT

Two weeks before Christmas last year, my friend Flynn and I were on our way back from Wyoming on highway 80 when something happened that was one of the most profound experiences of my life. We were about a half hour out of Rawlins, in the middle of what I call "nowhere land" when we noticed several crows flying erratically, swooping and diving and harassing a huge golden eagle. They were all tussling and making such a huge commotion in the sky. And then "Boom!" The eagle hit a passing semi at top speed and plummeted to the ground. We saw him hit the side of the road and my friend slammed on the brakes so fast, my completely full latte flew out of my hands and splattered onto the windshield as we skidded to a stop. When we caught our breath, we drove in reverse until we were parked behind the eagle, so we could be a windshield for oncoming traffic.

Flynn got out of the truck first. "Oh, love. I think he's dying." I could hear his voice through my open window. I got out of the truck and walked over to them. Such a huge and majestic bird. I was instantly struck by the beauty of his feathers and the sheer size of him. I had never been so close to a bird that big. One wing was bent out to the side and his left leg was in front of him. Head down, I could see he had blood coming out of his beak. "Oh my God! We have to do something!" I stated.

Flynn went back to the truck to call the forestry service or wildlife rescue, anyone he could get ahold of on a Sunday morning. I stayed with the bird. I was in awe of his beauty. The wind moved through his feathers at times and I could see the stunning layers and the subtlety of the different colors. I thought of how his morning must have been before this and imagined seeing through his eyes as he flew above the treetops, feeling the morning sun on his outstretched wings; the freedom he must have felt in his soul being able to soar in the sky and float among the clouds. My heart ached to see him lying in a heap at the side of the road now.

When I went back to the truck, Flynn had found a ranger who was on his way. "Do you want to stay?," he asked. "The ranger should be here in an hour or so. I know you have a lot to do when we get back home and I am sure they will find him." I burst into huge tears and sobbed, "I'm not leaving that bird!" We both agreed it was the best thing to stay with him.

We took turns going out of the truck to be with him. Right away I began to pray, still sobbing uncontrollably. For some reason this hit the deepest parts of my heart, signifying the preciousness of all of life. I dropped into the center of my soul and just kept sending him love. At one point the eagle pulled in its wing and tucked his leg back underneath him. Head still down, he looked like he was nesting, sleeping there with his eyes closed at the side of the road.

And then, out of the blue, he opened his eyes, raised his head, and began looking around. He didn't move anything else. We assumed his wing was broken and that he was bleeding internally. He slowly looked around and then our eyes met. From inside my heart I said to him, "It's okay. Help is on the way. You're safe." I felt he understood. He seemed calm, just lying there taking it all in. Several times we locked eyes and I continued to send him the same message. I felt our souls connect and our hearts beat in rhythm.

After an hour and a half, the ranger showed up. From where I sat in the truck still making contact with the bird, I could hear the ranger's conversation with Flynn. "We are going to have to get this coat around him," he said. "We'll take him to the raptor rescue where they will be able to take care of him. He'll be in captivity the rest of his life, but at least he will be alive." And as if the eagle was listening to their conversation, no sooner than those words were out of the ranger's mouth, the eagle suddenly jumped to its feet. He looked around for a split second and then "Whoosh!" He spread out his six feet of grand wingspan, and ascended into the sky.

"Holy sh*t!" We all exclaimed at once. The eagle circled around the truck once as a final farewell and then in his effortless majesty, soared up across the road and into the hills nearby. We watched him in silent awe until he was only a speck of dark sand in the sky. We had witnessed what appeared to be a death, and then the resurrection from it. We knew we had just witnessed a miracle; this eagle refusing to go into captivity and the triumph of his spirit awakening and taking flight. As I watched him fade into the horizon, a distinct speck in the landscape of the sky, I had a deep knowingness that his heart was within me, and in his freedom, my own heartbeat with a sacred and timeless rhythm where we are all intimately connected and in our oneness, we are all free.

THE DIVINE INSIDE

Gregg Braden is a *New York Times* best-selling author, scientist, and internationally renowned pioneer in bridging science, spirituality and the real world. In one of his interviews I listened to he said, "We don't have to do anything to become enlightened and aware. We already *are* it. We just need to let go of the mind and our emotions and relax into our true nature which is love." How is your fear of death transformed when you are aware of your own divinity? It is by embracing your divinity that you transcend fear. When you acknowledge that you are a part of the everlasting spark of the Divine, then you can relax into your expression of that spark in this world, the same spark that was in the eagle at the side of the road, knowing that your light continues on.

In his book, *The God Code*, Gregg says, "We are God eternal in the body…Divinity has nothing to do with religion. Our ability to transcend perceived human limitations…it's about accessing that part of ourselves that is veiled by fear." You can make a difference in this world, not by trying to get others to believe what you believe, but by being a living example of what it feels like to live with your embodied divinity.

Living with embodied divinity means you are a light unto others, that you live through your conscious loving heart, and you recognize the divinity in yourself and all others regardless of their behaviors, beliefs, or lifestyle choices. Each soul is on their own divine path. It is not up to you to determine what is right for everyone else, it is your responsibility to awaken the deeper knowing of your divinity so you can help shine that light on those who still live in the dark. You can access that divinity in this moment by closing your eyes and concentrating on your heart. This is where you and the Divine entwine. Be still and just notice.

The great spiritual teacher Ram Dass reminds us, "Everyone you meet is, in their spirit, the same as you. Underneath the wrappings of name, form, beliefs, etc, there is only consciousness. And that consciousness is the same for everybody — every soul experiences life, and every heart craves joy. Not only are we all consciousnesses the same in this way, but we are also deeply interconnected. Because we share the world, what affects one consciousness affects all of them."

In speaking about death, Ram Dass writes, "Ramana Maharshi was a great Indian saint. When he was dying of cancer, his devotees said, "Let's treat it." And Ramana Maharshi said, "No, it is time to drop this body." His devotees started to cry. They begged him,

"Bhagwan, don't leave us, don't leave us!" And he looked at them with confusion and said, "Don't be silly. Where could I possibly go?" You know, it's almost like he was saying, "Don't make such a fuss. I'm just selling the old family car."

These bodies we live in, and the ego that identifies with it, are just like the old family car. They are functional entities in which our Soul travels through our incarnation. But when they are used up, they die. The most graceful thing to do is to just allow them to die peacefully and naturally – to "let go lightly." As Ram Das says, "Through it all, who we are is Soul. When the body and the ego are gone, the Soul will live on, because the Soul is eternal. Eventually, in some incarnation, when we've finished our work, our Soul can merge back into the One . . . back into God . . . back into the Infinite."

TALKING TO GOD

When I spoke to Neale Donald Walsch about his new book, *God Talks*, I loved the important message that he shared that, "Everyone is having a conversation with God, but we're simply calling it something else because we don't want to be marginalized or ridiculed or made fun of. Our culture disapproves that God is talking directly to us." He went on to point out that God doesn't just talk to a bishop or a priest. He said, "All of us are having conversations with God all the time but we call it something else, 'women's intuition, a coincidence, a psychic hit, an epiphany,' whatever words we can use to describe that exact same phenomenon."

This is so vitally important; the knowledge that you are not separate from God (the Divine, in whatever term you use.) You can talk to God directly and when you are quiet enough, you will hear the stirrings of your soul, or find specific signs directly guiding you, or you will get direct downloads (inspired ideas) that come straight from the Divine. God is within you and is as close as your breath. Feel into your heart. It beats with the eternal rhythm of the universe to which you are infinitely connected.

What are your conversations with God like? Do you experience the Divine in signs, or internal knowings, or direct messages in dreams? What would it take for you to stop doubting this connection and allow yourself to experience it more fully? When you embrace the thought that you are inseparable from the Divine spark that created you and is in you, that connection becomes something that is an innate part of you that you can access in any given moment. This is an important part of what can alleviate your fear of death.

TAPPING IN:

1. Take a few moments to drop your attention from your head into your heart. Place your hand on your heart and breathe into that space and notice the connection you have to love. The Divine *is* love. That love you feel in you is the Divine in action. Allow it to activate and radiate through your heart. Then imagine that energy and sense of connection going out to those you love, both living and on the other side. Keep breathing into this space and allowing that deep sense of connection to radiate and resonate within you. Love connects us to the Divine inside of us, each other, and eternity. This love never ends.

2. What have your experiences of the sacred been? Think about how you might best connect with these sacred experiences as you bring them to mind now. You could write them down, draw or paint a picture representing them, or create a song (even if you only sing it to yourself) that allows you to anchor to the sacred within you even more fully.

3. Begin to focus on your access to the Divine. Ask God (or your Higher Power) questions about death, life, and the afterlife, and like Neale, write down your answers. Be open to that still soft voice inside of you guiding you to the answers and the eternity of your soul.

Chapter Four:
Extended Journeys

"The grave itself is but a covered bridge, leading
from light to light, through a brief darkness!"
-HENRY WADSWORTH LONGFELLOW

Exploring our shared stories of loss and our experiences of continued life are vital. I have heard these stories from countless other people throughout my lifetime. Right after the incident that day in the bathtub when my daughter Acacia talked to me about my "other mother Dorothy," I was in a local shop here in old town Fort Collins when for some reason, as I was checking out of the store, the clerk and I started talking (and talking, and talking.)

During our extended conversation, I ended up sharing the amazing story of what had just happened to me and my daughter talking about being a light up in the sky with God. She looked at me with a knowing smile, "You may know my husband," she said. He was a local doctor at The Children's Clinic in town. She shared that he had had many experiences with his patients who were children, sharing stories from where they had been before being on this plane of existence. But none of them, she said, were as powerful as what they had just heard from their own son, who was ironically, like Acacia, only four years old at the time. "One day, just after breakfast, he just began to talk about God," she shared. "He said he and several other people were up in the sky with God and that they all looked like the lights on the end of birthday candles."

Wow! Lights in the sky. I couldn't believe it! It was such validation for what I had just experienced with my daughter. It was only the first of hundreds of other stories I would hear from others throughout my lifetime; stories that differ in content but are consistent with their message that our souls go on.

Twenty three years later, I was standing on a mountain top overlooking the Great Salt Lakes watching the sunset on the horizon when the timeless sense of connection occurred. I had experienced that connectedness several times throughout my life, but this one was so powerful for me, I have carried it as a vivid reminder in my pocket of memories, to pull out when I need to pause, breathe deep, and remember the never-ending web of life we are all connected to.

It was a couple of weeks after I had heard about the terminal diagnosis my aunt Gwen had received, although when I was first standing at the top of the mountain, I wasn't even thinking about her. Then, as the sun began to set and the sky was ablaze with color, and the night sky began to sprinkle stars, I felt her. I was distinctly aware of her essence. I could feel her throughout my being and the pure, radiant, and eternal spirit of her wrapped around me like a warm blanket holding me close to her.

Then I felt my heart begin to soar up into the sky and connect with the fading sunlight and felt that light was radiating out to all of my loved ones. Like waves, the connections of their spirits to mine, came to me and through me. I couldn't move, only breathe in the wonder of the moment. I could feel my parents, my grandparents both living and past, my precious daughter Acacia, and my dear friends. And then like a firework it expanded into the sky, the stars, and the sea of everything that was living (which was everything!) The rocks, the grass, the trees… everything seemed illuminated, glowing with divine energy connecting us all. I had stepped into the oneness of the mystery. The oneness that is available to all of us because it *is* us.

Just take a deep breath on that. "We are all connected and our souls go on eternally." Allow yourself to marinate on that thought for a few moments. See what you notice within you. Is there a sense of lightness or expansion within you? Pay attention to how your body responds as you feel into those words. Feel into your heart and your connection to your own spirit and then the connection you feel to others that transcends space and time. What do you think would happen if you started to trust life (and death) as your greatest allies on this journey, as mere portals to your ever-expanding experience of the great mystery. When you realize that this life-death-life cycle is just a part of the whole plan, you can begin to more fully trust the Divine Orchestrator, who created it all.

When you befriend the present moment as showing up perfectly as it is, you let go of the need to control things and you are able to let go of your fear of the future as well. Death will be a part of your life too. A divine pause before rebirth into the next expression of the spark that is your eternal soul's journey. This moment is your opportunity to practice this sacred alliance with all that is, and surrender to the eternal "now" which will create profound freedom in your life. As you drop into this space, you drop into the expansiveness of eternity and let go of fear, for there is only ever "right now."

LIGHT FROM BEYOND

The National Library of Medicine and the National Center for Biotechnology Information have reported their research results from 2001-2008 from an ongoing nationwide survey of older adults and their contact with the dead. This survey helped look at how this contact lowered death anxiety for the participants who had experienced contact with a loved one who had passed. Approximately 73% of the participants in this study reported that they felt as though a loved one who has died is looking over them at least once in a while, 48.7% indicated they felt a dead loved one was in the same room at least once in a while, 23.9% said they heard the voice of a dead loved one at least once in a while, and 20.7% stated that they actually see a dead loved one at least once in a while. Consistent with the findings from other studies (Klugman 2006), this data suggests that having contact with the dead is a fairly common experience. Perhaps the veil is thinning and your ability to feel, see, and experience those loved ones who have passed and your connection to them is more available than you realized.

RETURNING TO LOVE

Chelsea is a profound healer. It is palpable when you meet her and stunning to find out she grew up not feeling seen, heard, or nurtured emotionally. Although her parents were both C.E.O.s, very successful, and charismatic outside of the home, inside of it, they were both incredibly narcissistic and cruel and Chelsea's childhood was fraught with verbal abuse and a lot of gutting emotional pain.

At 33 and living in North Carolina, far away from her parents in California, Chelsea was cultivating a wonderful life for herself.

Her professional career was expanding and she was living a life of service by helping others heal. She and a dear friend decided to collaborate, create, and host a Gnosis event in Los Angeles, where they could serve a large group of people in intuitive breathwork, vocal toning, and movement.

The event was a huge success, helping hundreds of people. Afterward, Chelsea stayed in the L.A. area for a few days. While there, one evening she decided to go to church and was inspired to drive by her childhood home and pray for her parents. Unbeknownst to her, her mother was in the hospital at the time having a tummy tuck and hernia surgery. She recalled how wild it was to find out that the next day, while she was getting her haircut back in L.A., that her mother had died suddenly from a blood clot in the hospital just three blocks away from the salon where Chelsea was sitting.

The serendipity that happened was stunning. Chelsea and her friend had organized the Gnosis event in L.A. *six months earlier,* and she hadn't spoken to her parents in years so she had no idea that her mother was having a routine surgery. Chelsea had driven clear across the country for an event she was called to do in her heart, not knowing she would be the closest living relative by proximity to her mother when she died unexpectedly and suddenly only three blocks away.

Seven months after her mother's death, she attended her mother's celebration of life back in Santa Barbara which happened to be hosted on her mother's birthday. It was tremendously difficult for Chelsea to walk into a room full of all of her mother and father's friends when she felt like she had been the black sheep of the family and labeled the "bad daughter" by her abusive parents. Chelsea showed up at the celebration fully in her heart to honor her mother and it was in that action that something deeply shifted.

Three months later, she felt the energy of her mother in her field of awareness. When she spoke to a friend who was a medium about this her friend said, "Your mother is here and she is a hoot!" She also told Chelsea that her mother was in a guide school because she had a lot of cleanup to do. As time continued, Chelsea began to feel her mother more fully in her awareness. She began to experience her as a frequency of joy and could feel her mother's pure essence coming through. Her mother's pure soul frequency evaporated any past trauma, karma, or ancestral baggage she had carried and the pure love that was her true essence showered onto Chelsea in a deeply healing way.

Chelsea began to viscerally feel her mother's pure love and care and was able to see her mother through her inner vision. Her mother told her, "I chose to die now so you could fully bloom." Chelsea felt that when her mother died, she had been given a part of her soul back that had felt robbed from her as a child. In the last two years since her mother passed, Chelsea has become a phenomenal conduit for love, healing, and Divine connection, assisting hundreds of others to tap into their souls, heal their hearts, and discover their wholeness in profound ways. Her mother's gift beyond death has opened up unimaginable gifts in Chelsea, and through those gifts, Chelsea now blesses the rest of the world.

Even if you don't share a positive relationship with someone in this life, in the realm of spirit, the love can still come through and remain in a way that maybe it wasn't able to be communicated while the person was living. Death can become a new chapter in the relationship book of your life. When you open to the possibility of this, you may begin to notice the synchronicities, signs and signals that your loved one has never fully left, but has kept loving you, in a new pure and refined way from beyond.

CHAPTER FOUR: EXTENDED JOURNEYS

THE LEGACY LIVES ON

I have been impacted deeply by the life and death of many people. Amazingly, the lessons I learned from the late Wayne Dyer became even more profound after his passing. I had the joy of meeting Wayne in Colorado in 2006, when he was on his tour speaking about his latest book at the time, *Change Your Thoughts–Change Your Life: Living the Wisdom of the Tao*. I was there with my mother and step-father who both loved him and were avid followers of his work. My step-father and I had discussions about Wayne when I was a teenager, as his book *Your Erroneous Zones* had changed my step-dad's life paradigm. At one point, when one of our family members had a huge personal struggle in their life that affected us all, I bought everyone in my family a copy of Wayne's book, *Inspiration*, and through our shared conversations around the book, it truly helped us all pull through a very difficult time together.

When I was at Wayne's event with my parents, there was an intermission half way through where he allowed people to come up to the front where he was signing books. There were about 5,000 people in the audience at the event center. I told my mother, "Come with me! We are going to meet him." She replied, "Stephanie, there are so many people! There is no way we are going to make it up there before we have to go back to our seats." I stood up, and gently took her hand and walked down into the massive crowd that had gathered to meet him. Walking forward, I knew I would speak with him.

As I am sure many people did, I felt his books had spoken directly to my heart at times and that I had a heart connection with him, but what happened next was seriously one of the wildest things I have experienced! As my mother and I walked through the crowd, it was like the parting of the Red Sea. It was as if hundreds and hundreds of people knew we were on our way to meet Wayne and they just cleared the path for us. We walked right up to the front of the line without cutting in front of anyone.

There was only one woman ahead of us and as she turned to leave, Wayne looked down at me (he is very tall) and my heart was so full, I blurted out, "I just love you!" He smiled and laughed and wrapped his arms around me in a warm embrace and said, "I love you too!" and gave me a kiss on the cheek. Such a beautiful moment. My mom stood there in disbelief with a huge smile on her face. Like so many millions of people, he touched my heart and my family's life in many ways.

I was stunned to hear the news nine years later that he had passed. I literally heard it from a very close source who was dear friends with Wayne's assistant Dee, who was the one who had discovered him dead from a heart attack. I felt as if I had lost someone very close to me.

Meeting Wayne's youngest child, Saje, just recently, was a profound and beautiful moment in my life. She and I had already scheduled an interview on my podcast to discuss her and her sister Serena's new book, *The Knowing*. Through my work on Humanity's Team I knew Saje and her family had continued to have contact with Wayne even after he had passed. Saje and Serena have a master class on the platform discussing this connection. When I reached out to Saje to see if she would be willing to jump on a separate call to discuss the connection beyond this life to her father, her reply was, "I'd love to!" Saje has such a lovely presence. She is solid, articulate, open, and kind.

She shared first about her wonderful childhood and the joyful experience of having two very laid back parents that allowed her to fully bloom into herself without putting any conditions on her to be something *they* wanted. Saje said, "Of course you had to have manners, put effort into being positive and being a good person, but you were allowed the freedom to pursue your own passions." Although her parents were separated when she was eleven, she stated that after a short while, her parents went back to being best friends, talking on the phone everyday, taking family vacations together and spending holidays together as a family.

Saje was very close to her father. She shared that even though he had moved to Maui and Saje and her siblings lived in Florida, Wayne came back to Florida a lot to see them, and they all spent the summers in Maui together. Saje said there never was a feeling of lack or disconnection.

During the summer of 2015, Saje spent the summer with Wayne on his tour to Australia and New Zealand. She recalls how wonderful the time was with her dad and her sister Skye. Saje spoke for fifteen minutes on stage with her dad at these events and her sister Skye would sing on stage as well. It was a wonderful time of connection for all of them. Wayne was so full of life and loving what he did best; connecting with and helping others. Saje said there was no way she could have ever expected the phone call that came two days after she returned from New Zealand, telling her that her vibrant and loving father was dead.

The next couple of weeks were very hard for Saje. She said, "At first I questioned everything he had ever told me about being a spiritual person having a human experience and that there was life after death." "I became a skeptical believer looking for proof for a period of a time." Saje said the proof actually got there very quickly. Within a couple of weeks she was getting dreams and undeniable signs. In the first week of her grief after her dad had passed, she said she would find herself grieving in the shower thinking, "I can never call him again!" One morning that first week after saying this again to herself, she heard him speaking in her head saying, "Yes, you will never call me again. That is the reality of life and death. But you know you have the tools within you. You have a lifetime of knowing me. You have ways to reach me."

After that, Saje began to ask for him to visit her in her dreams. Two or three weeks later, she was asleep in her apartment in New York. When her alarm went off that morning, she hit the snooze button and immediately fell back asleep. In her sleep state she was exactly where she was in real life. She could see that she was right there in her bed, holding her phone that had her alarm on it.

In her dream, she heard someone walk in through the front door of the apartment and she got up out of bed to go see who it was. It was her dad, walking into her apartment with a big grin on his face. "He was not wearing a shirt," she said, "In life, he was never wearing a shirt living on Maui." He walked in with almost a smirk on his face like he was really pleased with himself and thought it was really funny. Saje said to him, "What are you doing here? Are you really here?" And Wayne replied, "I'm really here." Saje said to herself, "I know I'm asleep but this is not a dream." Her dad said, "This isn't a dream. This is real." Saje responded, "Ok, if you're really here, then I can touch you." "So touch me," Wayne replied and reached out his arms. Saje reached out her hands and touched him.

They talked for a while and then Saje said it turned into an actual dream where she was with her dad and her brothers in a pool that felt different than when she was first talking with her dad. Then Saje's alarm went off again and she knew being with her dad in the apartment wasn't a dream at all. She told me, "It was more real than anything."

That weekend Saje went to her father's public celebration of life and met psychic medium Karen Noe. Earlier, Karen had been talking to Serena, Saje's sister, asking about whether she had had any contact with her father. "Just so you'll know that it is a real visitation, two things will happen," Karen told her. "One is if there is lucid dreaming and the other is the acknowledgement of or invitation to touch." Serena replied, "Oh my God! My sister Saje hasn't shut up about this dream she had and those are the two things she keeps focusing on, that they touched and although she was dreaming, she knew it wasn't a dream!" When Serena told Sage about her conversation with Karen, that was all the validation Saje needed to know that her experience was real.

In my personal conversation with Saje, she shared with me that she had two beautiful children and that something just recently had happened with her five-year-old son, Julian, who had convinced her of this connection with her father even further. Saje shared that she and her husband sleep with their children, Saje with their two-year-old and her husband with Julian. Saje said that one night her husband was out of town so Saje and both of her children all slept together. That night something powerful and profound happened.

In the middle of the night, Saje was awakened by the sound of weeping. It was coming from Julian. She asked, "Julian are you ok? Are you feeling sick?" He said, "No." but he was sniffling and crying. Saje felt his cheeks and they were wet with tears. She cuddled him closely thinking he was probably just missing his dad who he was used to sleeping with. When they woke up the next morning, Saje asked Julian, "Why were you crying in the middle of the night?" He said, "I was just missing your father, my grandfather." They had never met. Wayne had passed five years before Julian was born. Saje asked, "You were missing him? What do you mean? Do you remember him?" "No," he replied, "I just miss him."

Saje said that it was very unlike Julian to act that way because he was not an overly emotional child and that already at five, he felt embarrassed to cry. That morning when Julian was sharing that he missed her father, he began to cry again. It was so special for Saje to witness her son's tenderness with her father and hi remarkable and real connection to him. Julian's connection with Wayne is really beautiful and beyond regular explanation. Saje also shared that during the last two years, her mother, Marcelene, has done a couple of ayahuasca ceremonies where she connected with Wayne as well. In one of those ceremonies, she had a vision that she shared with Saje. She said that Wayne came to her and she asked him, "Are you coming back in another life?" And Wayne had shown her Julian. Marcelene asked, "You're Julian?" He said, "Yes." Then Marcelene asked, " Will he continue all your work?" And then Wayne showed her all of his work on a bookshelf and then it disappeared as if to signify, "No, my work is done."

Saje said she doesn't know if her father is really Julian, but when Julian was weeping and she thought of how many personality traits of his were like her fathers, it opened her up to that possibility. I shared with Saje my experience of Acacia at four years old and her speaking to me about the light of my "other mother Dorothy" being put in her light and that maybe Julian was his own soul with his own light and that some of Wayne's light was in him too. "Yes! I love that!" she replied, lit up after I had shared this with her. "I like the idea of him just being my son and also having my part of my dad in him as well."

CHAPTER FOUR: EXTENDED JOURNEYS

SOUL SISTERS

Unfortunately, Saje has gone through the grief of losing another family member besides her father. She shared with me that two years ago, her sister Sommer had passed after a long struggle with drug addiction. Saje's sister Serena shared Sommer's passing beautifully in this Facebook post. Serena writes, "My sister Sommer Wayne Dyer passed away yesterday. I just saw her this past week. I was in Costa Rica where she lived, and was just with her. Sommer has always been a person like no one else I have ever known. The funniest, wittiest, brightest person alive. I cannot believe she is not here anymore. I know she is with me, with all of our siblings and mom and family, and I also know she is flying high with my dad and her son Haze. Heartbroken doesn't describe it. She loved so fiercely, she never hesitated to tell all of us how much she loves us, and we in turn never hesitated to shower her in our love as well. I feel like a part of me is gone now. She was the only sibling whose photo I carried in my wallet for years and years. I love her so, so much and I will miss her all the days of my life. My Sommer, my sister, my Gayle. The person I followed around like I was her shadow when we were toddlers. She is my lighthouse. Her light, her laugh, always brought me home. And will continue to do so, now just from the other side."

Saje said Sommer's death at thirty two was a totally different grief than her father's because Sommer was so young and her father had lived a whole life. She shared that these two losses have totally shifted her perspective on life.

Saje and I were having this conversation over a zoom call where she had gone downstairs from her apartment and into the gym area where she could sit by some windows and we could talk uninterrupted. As we were talking about Sommer, all of the sudden Saje paused and said, "Oh my God!" and stopped the conversation to better listen to something. "What's going on?" I asked. "I can't believe it!" she said. "The song that is playing in this gym right now, is the song that my sister sang at Sommer's funeral." "We chose this song, *True Colors*, because it reminded us all so much of her!."

The instrumental version of the song was playing in the gym that she frequented, that she had never heard played there before. I said, " Maybe your sister is here too?" "Yeah," Saje answered, "My whole body is shaking." "So you wanted to talk about signs," she said, "Here you go."

It is clear that these experiences are not something that just happen to some of us, but something that can be experienced by all of us. It is powerful when we share our stories about these connections beyond death. Perhaps if we continue this practice of expanding our connections to those who have passed and open up these conversations, we normalize this shared experience and create doorways for clearer communication and a deeper understanding of our lives and our connection to the mystery of it all. When this happens, our anxieties are dispelled, our consciousness is expanded and we step into a greater sense of coherence with life itself and the sacredness of life beyond life as well.

TAPPING IN:

1. What are your experiences with life after life? Do you have a sense that you have been here before or had a glimpse into any of your own past lives? Has anyone from the other side ever come to you in a dream, vision, or as a distinct voice heard within your heart? Keep a dream journal beside your bed and upon waking, record any dreams or messages you have received.

2. We talked about saying what you need to say to people while they are living. Who do you want to make sure you connect with and what is important to you to say to them? Start writing that letter and explore how you can best share it with them. If they have already passed you can still write a letter and read that letter out loud to them. It will still be received.

3. Watch a film that positively portrays connection with the other side, *Ghost*, *About Time*, and *Coco* are a few that come to mind that have touched my heart and reassured me that what I know in my soul is true. Our souls continue on.

Chapter Five:
We are Never Alone

> "Ghosts are all around us. Look for them, and you will find them. Our feet are planted in the real world, but we dance with angels and ghosts."
> –RUSKIN BOND

I have always wondered why it was ok for us to accept that angels appear in the bible (KJV says 285 times) but if someone says they experienced an angel or a spirit today, it is still considered taboo, or fringey, or strange. I remember reading a book a long time ago that stated if we were able to see all the angels and spirits around us, it would fill the room.

I have never been one to believe in "ghosts" and I have never liked that word, as it always felt like it implied something scary to be feared. As a therapist, the stories I have heard over the last three decades of spirit or angel encounters are far too many to count. Even people who seem very conservative or are in career positions where they might not ever dare to mention their experiences for fear of backlash, have shared their stories in the safety of my office walls.

If you accept that life continues on after death, could you also accept that seeing, hearing, or experiencing spirits might be a possibility; one that isn't scary or weird, but normalized and accepted as your continued connection with the emanating light of your and your loved ones' souls?

THE LIGHTS AT MY DOOR

For me, one of the most profound experiences of seeing what I would consider an actual spirit was at my mother's house. She hates it when I tell this story because she doesn't like people to think her house is haunted. It is not haunted. However, there have definitely been some interesting phenomena and interactions with spirits there that have been experienced by me and several others who have visited her home.

My mother's home is a place of connection and loved by my large, wonderful family that gathers there for all of our holidays. It is also a place where the veil is thin and some very interesting and profound things have happened that have assured me and several others that death is just a doorway and that sometimes it opens from the other side.

I can't tell you when it started. I just know that as a child, it went on until I left my family home at age thirteen. There were several nights when I would awaken, and three illuminated figures would be there standing in the doorway to my room in the dark. Two little, one big. Not ghosts, nothing I could see clearly, just energy imprints, outlines of some kind of figures just glowing in the hallway. I wasn't really afraid. I honestly didn't know what to think of them. At some point, I just started unconsciously shutting and locking my door at night and the lights stopped appearing.

You might just write this up as the overactive imagination of a child. Maybe. And I may have written this all off as some kind of altered dream state I had experienced as a child as well, except that in the back of my mind, the memories were always so vivid that I knew what I had experienced was real.

Twenty years later, while I was picking up my ten-year-old daughter from spending a weekend at my mother's home, she said to me, "Mom, I had something weird happen at grandma's last night." "Oh, what happened?" I asked. "Well, in the middle of the night, these light people were standing at my door." I drew in a breath. "Yeah, there were three of them. One big and two little."

My friends and I often say, "Truth is stranger than fiction," and when moments like this happen, we look at each other and laugh and say, "You just can't make this sh*t up!" Whatever my daughter and I experienced was real. Who's to say what it "really" was, only that the energy that was in my mother's home when I was a child was still there decades later, furthering my belief that there is something more here for us than just this flesh and bones existence that we experience during waking hours. As an adult, I have never encountered that light at my mother's again, but I am convinced it happened both to my daughter and to me and what we both experienced was something very, very real.

One of the most profound experiences with the other side happened when my youngest daughter Hailey was about seven years old. We lived in Wyoming and she and my older daughter Acacia and I had come down to Fort Collins for Thanksgiving that year. My cousin's son, Tommy, had stayed at my mother's house the night before we got there in the guest room downstairs. He happily moved over to my grandfather's house, who lived a few blocks away, the night we arrived so we could stay in the guest bedroom at mom's. That night, Acacia said she was going to stay up and watch movies with her favorite female cousin and Hailey and I went to bed. It had been a long day and we both fell fast asleep. A couple of hours later, I was awakened by what

I thought was her at the end of the bed. I looked up and saw a little girl standing there. "Hailey, what do you need, honey?" I asked. The actual Hailey, who was still sleeping beside me, stirred in her sleep. "Oh, my God!" I exclaimed to myself, "It's a ghost!"

I am embarrassed to tell you, but at that moment, fear overtook me and I ran out of the bedroom, leaving my seven-year-old daughter in the room. Acacia and her cousin were still watching movies, and losing my breath, I stammered, "There was a little girl in there with us! A ghost!" We all squealed and that's when I realized I needed to get back in there with Hailey. She hadn't awakened and was still lying there peacefully, no ghost in sight.

I prayed with all of my might, "Dear God please protect us. Put your golden light around us and keep us safe." With that, a calm came over me and my breathing slowed until I finally fell back asleep. An hour and a half later, it happened again. I opened my eyes and again, the little girl was standing there at the end of the bed. I ran back out of the room once more, shouting to the two girls that were still up, "She's in there again!" We half laughed at the thought of it and the reality that something was indeed appearing in that room. We all went into the room and again, no little girl but Hailey was there. I am not sure how I got back to sleep that night. I just know, I held Hailey tight and prayed the love of God would surround and protect us.

The next morning Tommy and my grandfather came over for breakfast and we were all sitting around the table when Tommy said, "I have to tell you. I had the weirdest thing happen when I spent the night over here the other night." We all looked at one another with eyes wide. "The darndest thing, I don't know if I was dreaming or what, but I got up in the middle of the night to go to the bathroom and there was a little girl standing at the end of the bed. It about scared me to death!" The girls and I all squealed! "No way!" I said, "That is exactly what happened to me last night, twice!" Tommy was a conservative farm kid who didn't believe in such things, but we all knew, as we shared our biscuits and gravy that morning, that something beyond our belief had happened.

Since then, several others have seen the little girl in the basement. Acacia shared with me years later that she had fallen asleep on the couch in the downstairs living room watching T.V. and said that she was covered in a blanket to keep warm. She was awakened when she started to feel footsteps walking over her on the couch. Acacia stated that there was no one there she could physically see, but that she knew it was the same little girl and that her feeling was that this little spirit was harmless and just wanted to play.

I can imagine how this all might land with you if you think spirits aren't real. You don't have to believe anything different than what you already believe. I am sharing this experience because there is something very powerful here. My *family* experienced something that none of us could explain, but enough of us experienced it, we couldn't doubt its authenticity. What is remarkable to me about this story is that it was a first hand experience of a different realm. A life after death.

I am not an expert on ghosts or paranormal experiences. I'm not even a novice in these areas besides the experiences that I have shared. What I do know, is that it is a common occurrence that is not to be feared. We are connected to a Divine source and we don't have to fear what shows up in the dark. Bringing in the light of the Divine and a sense of love to our hearts, we can cast out any shadows and invite them to return to the light.

CHAPTER FIVE: WE ARE NEVER ALONE

STORIES FROM BEYOND

When I think of how the Divine works with us and for us, I think of the many years in my private practice. I cannot begin to tell you the number of times a client has told me, "God just led me to you." I always smile and say, "Thank you," with a knowingness in my heart that it is true. I do believe the Divine guides us to one another for our deepest lessons and greatest healing. There are no mistakes.

One of these wonderful clients who had shared that she felt guided to my office was a beautiful woman doing grief work over her marriage that was ending and trying to heal the pain it had caused her by staying in an unhealthy relationship for so long. As with many clients that have experienced some sort of trauma, we decided a good course of treatment would be E.M.D.R. (This is a trauma protocol, with over 35 years of empirical research that proves how it neurologically rewires trauma held in the brain and physiologically restores the person to a regulated state of being.)

There have been many times over my last seventeen years of utilizing the profound healing protocol of E.M.D.R. where I have noticed a certain kind of light that seemed to emanate from someone as they went through the healing process. It might be a change in their eyes or a bright light that seemed to radiate around their heads as they healed that always caught my attention. Frequently, after such a session, my clients would tell me they felt "lighter" or that when they opened their eyes after treatment, things looked brighter and not quite the same.

That day, my client was in the last phase of E.M.D.R., the phase where the trauma disturbance level has been reduced to zero when recalling the traumatic event and the client then focuses on the installation of positive thoughts. For some reason, I decided to close my eyes as she was completing this phase of treatment. I usually keep my eyes open while the client is going through each 90-second set of bilateral stimulation so I can watch their face for signs of how they are processing and can encourage them through the process.

As I closed my eyes, I became aware I could see two figures, surrounded by light sitting down on either side of her on the couch. I slowly opened my eyes and saw my client sitting there alone, so I closed my eyes again, and the two figures were still there. I had a deep sense that these beings were my client's parents, there supporting her in her healing. They were radiating with such incredible love for their daughter. Such a pure and palpable love, it completely washed over the room and filled my heart. Then, I heard an inner voice say, "I am her father." I was in disbelief. I had never had anything like this happen to me. "It's just my imagination," I said to myself. I heard a little chuckle and then, "No, this is real. I am her father. I used to be an avid fisherman." And then I kept hearing the word "sprockets" and I had no idea what that word meant. I didn't know what a sprocket was.

I opened my eyes to check on my client. The whole thing happened in a matter of five seconds, but it felt timeless and his voice that I had heard internally, sounded as real as anyones I had ever experienced externally. When I checked in with her then and asked her what she had noticed, she said, "I just have the sense that my mom and dad are here with me." I froze. Holy sh*t! It was real! I was overwhelmed with emotions. Not wanting to disturb her process, we continued the session until it was completed. The trauma in the area of her relationship was resolved and she said she had a profound sense of peace in her heart.

Before she got up to leave, at the risk of her thinking that her therapist had gone crazy and her never wanting to return,

I said, "I'd like to share something I experienced today while you were doing your work." I told her about the lights and that I had perceived them sitting beside her right before she told me she felt like her parents were there. "Oh my goodness!" she exclaimed. She said that both of her parents had passed over fifteen years ago and that she had truly felt them beside her during the E.M.D.R.. I told her, "I didn't really believe it and then your dad said something about being an avid fisherman." She began to weep. "That was the love of my father's life," she said, "and such a huge part of who he was." We exchanged a knowing look between us and both took a deep breath, breathing in the reality of what was happening. "There was one other thing," I said, "I kept hearing the word, 'sprockets.' I don't know if that means anything to you?" My client's eyes opened up wide and the tears continued to spill down her cheeks. "Oh. My. God." she exclaimed in almost a state of shock. "My father's job while I was growing up was to visit the local dairy farmers and help them fix their milking machines. When he was home my special time with him was to sit in his mechanic shop as he worked on the milkers. We were surrounded by sprockets. They were part of the machinery he replaced on those milking machines!" Huge body chills. My truth bumps showed up and the truth resonated through me. We embraced and she thanked me dearly for this gift of connecting to her parents. She said that she felt them both around her but had never had any "proof" like this, that they were really there beside her, holding her in their light as she healed.

REMEMBRANCE

I have known Tami for over a decade. Not only does she have one of the biggest hearts and most contagious laughs of anyone you could ever meet, she is also an entrepreneur and one of those women who can do anything from running a business and managing staff, to raising kids and remodeling her home. I have known her for all these years and it was just lately, while she was attending my women's retreat in Sayulita, Mexico, that she shared her amazing story with me.

Tami never really knew her grandfather. She was five years old when he passed away and she says she has very few memories of him other than that she knew he was kind. So, she was shocked a year ago, at the age of 57, when he showed up at the church service she was attending with her mother. Tami said she wasn't a religious person and was going to church to support her mother and spend time with her while she was visiting. She said she was sitting there listening to the sermon when she saw her grandfather standing up by the pulpit. She can describe him perfectly in his white shirt, black pants, and black tie-up shoes. Tami was sitting near the back of the church and started looking around to see if anyone else might be noticing what she was experiencing. No one seemed to notice him but her.

When she looked back up, he was looking right at her and started walking down the aisle towards where she was sitting. As he approached her, he stretched out his arms to her. Tammy said she didn't know what to do. He was so real she wondered if she should scoot over to make room for him to sit beside her. The love that she felt flowing from him with his outstretched hands was incredible. Tami said she was afraid to reach out and touch him but was then filled with a deep peace. She felt he had come to tell her that everything was ok and that she would be ok no matter what was happening in her life.

Tami looked at her mom to see if she was seeing what was happening and said that when she turned back to her grandfather, he was gone. The feeling of love remained. She knew his love and his being there with her was absolutely real. Tami shares this story with tears in her eyes. For a year she kept this story inside of her for fear that other people would think she was crazy. On the women's retreat, Tami experienced other people sharing their stories of connection with loved ones who had passed and she felt safe enough to share her experience and her truth.

When we begin to share our experiences, we find the beautiful common golden threads that connect us all. Tami felt validated in her experience and a huge relief in sharing her heart with others. What story do you have inside of you that longs to be shared? It is in the sharing of these stories that we create a new narrative of our shared human-spiritual journey and increase the consciousness of the planet. Your stories of experiencing connection from the other side are essential. Let's create a safe space within our hearts and with each other to share the serendipities, synchronicities, and sacred experiences that happen to us all.

WHAT HAPPENS NEXT DOOR

My cousin has lived next door to me for a decade in his grandmother's home. I had moved out of the state for a job after graduate school and had never spent much time with her, but enough to know that she was a woman full of joy who lived to take care of her family. When she passed, my cousin and his wife moved into the house and have shared that they are very aware that she is still there.

"Even before we had kids," my cousin shared, "we would hear footsteps above us when we were downstairs watching T.V." Since they have had children, they still hear her footsteps. My cousin said at night he and his wife will hear them and think that the kids are up out of bed messing around, only to find out when they go upstairs that the kids are fast asleep. "The presence of her is actually comforting," they have both said. "She is still here in her house, watching over us and taking care of us like she always did."

SPIRIT STORIES

Unfortunately, our society has sensationalized our connection to spirits with horror movies and reality TV shows about hunting ghosts. These forms of addressing spirits as something dark and scary perpetuates the fear narrative around death. Experiencing connection from those beyond death is actually amazingly common and one of the most normal things in the world. According to a recent YouGov poll, 67% of Americans polled said they have had a paranormal experience. 67%! That is almost two thirds of all Americans having experiences that they are not talking about. It is imperative that we start opening up this conversation and begin to validate one another's experiences instead of subscribing to a conditioned societal silence that tells us that these experiences are crazy. When we are able to authentically share our experiences with the paranormal we open up the potential for more meaningful encounters and connection on both sides of the veil.

If you shared your experiences with death and your encounters with life beyond death, think of the comfort that people would experience. It would help validate the beautiful message that sages have been trying to tell us for eons, that death is not the end. Think of the love and wisdom that could be shared if you were able to listen to your loved ones on the other side that were in their pure essence after having shed their personas, egos, and programming they were tied to in life. How might this inform your life and help you transcend your own traumas and tribulations?

There truly is another side to life that exists beyond death, even if you haven't seen it (yet.) The hundreds of people I have talked to that have shared their experiences are not crazy. We need to quit buying into the narrative that says if people's experiences are different from ours then "they" must be wrong. When these experiences have happened in my own life and to the hundreds of people I have spoken with, they have been profound and life changing moments. They open whole new worlds of connection and understanding. These encounters with a different dimension of beingness have been just as real for the people who have experienced them as the room you are sitting in right now as you read this book. Usually it is fear that keeps us from experiencing things. We are afraid of things we don't know, don't fully understand, or don't have a frame of reference for. We are also afraid to share experiences that might seem out of the norm. But what if this is the norm?

EVIDENCE OF ETERNITY

I had the distinct honor of connecting with the great Suzanne Giesemann. During our warm and wonderful conversation she shared stories that offered evidence and proof that death is not the end and that our loved ones beyond the veil are still with us.

What struck me as vital to understanding how powerful Suzanne's message is, is the fact that her earlier career was that of a Navy Commander. And not just any Navy Commander, mind you, but the aid to the Chairman of the Joint Chief of Staff, the nation's highest-ranking military officer and the principal military advisor to the president, the secretary of defense, and the National Security Council. She was in the last aircraft in the air when 9-11 happened and was escorted down by fighter jets to the Pentagon where she had to step over the rubble of the jet that had just flown into it once she had landed. All this to say, Suzanne is the real deal - solid, sane, and reliable. After 9-11, she retired after twenty years of military service, to the day, as she was so aware that life was too short to not be enjoying the fullness of it.

Years later when Suzanne's step-daughter, Susan was tragically killed by a lightning strike, her life was changed forever. She and her husband Ty went to see a medium to try and connect with Susan. The medium told them that a woman showed up in a brown uniform and had a little baby boy with her that she wanted to introduce to them. Suzanne and her husband were stunned. Susan was a Marine and was six months pregnant when she was killed. The medium went on to tell them that she could see Susan crawling up and sitting on her father's lap and leaning her head against him. Again, they were absolutely stunned. While this is something she had never done, as a 27 year old and a Marine, Susan had crawled into her father's lap and hugged him in this way the last time she saw him. It was the last time he saw her alive.

There was no doubt that this was real, and something that Suzanne refers to as, "N.O.E." No Other Explanation moments. It was the opening for her into her own experience as an extraordinary medium. After years of meditation, Suzanne began to lead classes on evidence-based mediumship, and became a world renowned medium. She has authored 13 books, has an award winning documentary, and was listed in *Watkins Mind Body Spirit Magazine*'s 2022 list of the 100 Most Spiritually Influential Living People.

Suzanne shared some of her profound experiences with me explaining that she rarely sees spirits but has a handful of times. She usually "sees" them in her mind's eye and then communicates with them internally. However, she told me about a time when a spirit appeared to her. She was having dinner with two people who were hosting an event she was presenting at. When they went out to dinner afterward, Suzanne told the couple, who had just lost a daughter and were wanting to do a reading with Suzanne the next day, that she didn't usually sense spirits in the material form.

Ironically during dinner, Suzanne saw a little girl with bunny ears on her head across the room and was aware it was a spirit. When she asked the couple if the little girl, she was experiencing with the bunny ears, was their daughter, they laughed. "Well, we used to call her our little rabbit. She had a little bunny rabbit figurine collection, and we used to photograph her in front of billboards with pictures of bunny rabbits!" It obviously *was* their daughter, showing up with bunny ears to let them know she was still their little rabbit.

Suzanne tenderly shared that when the mom came to the reading the next day, she brought one of her daughter's bunny figurines and gave it to Suzanne as a gift. Suzanne keeps that bunny right by her bathroom sink as a reminder that we can connect with the other side, that death is not the end, and that there is something more.

What is powerful about Suzanne's work is that she requires and insists on evidence from the spirits she is in contact with so there is specific proof for their loved ones still living. She said she and thousands of mediums use this method of insisting on evidence that there is no way they, as mediums would have access to, so they can share this proof with others. One of these evidence-based experiences occurred when a woman came for a reading and asked what her dead husband was doing now that he was in heaven. Suzanne heard from him, "I'm standing firmly on two feet, playing golf every day!" When she repeated this to his wife she gasped, "Golf was my husband's passion and the year before he died he had one of his legs amputated." In heaven, her husband wanted her to know he had both of his feet now and was playing his passion in the afterlife.

These are powerful stories that offer us all evidence, comfort, and proof that life continues on and we are truly connected throughout eternity. Just take a deep breath in and marinate on that thought for a moment: Life. Continues. On. Let it vibrate through your being and notice how your body begins to relax.

TAPPING IN:

1. Who has shown up as an angel in your life? Write down the people who have just "appeared" in your life and have been your guides or helped you in times when you really needed them. We have angels on both sides working for us.

2. What is your own experience of being in touch by the other side? Are there dreams you have had that you may have discounted that actually felt "real?" Or did you have experiences as a child that you wrote off as just having an "active imagination?" Write them down or audio record them. Who might you share these with?

3. Notice if there are parts of you that want to discount your experiences with the beyond. Ask these parts of you, "What are you afraid of if this event or experience was real?" Send love and compassion to these parts. They are just protective

parts trying to do their job to keep you from being hurt. Let them know, "Thank you for wanting to help me. I've got this. You can relax now. I am ready to move into a deeper truth."

Chapter Six:
Growing Through Grief

"Death is simply a shedding of the physical body, like the butterfly shedding its cocoon. It is a transition to a higher state of consciousness where you continue to perceive, to understand, to laugh, and to be able to grow."
–ELISABETH KUBLER-ROSS

I don't think we can just talk about death without discussing the grief that accompanies it. Even when we deeply understand that death is not the end, there is still loss, there is still an emptiness created when a loved one exits the stage of life. It's powerful to notice how your grief can also be transformed when you become more aware of your own divinity and that of your loved ones. You may deeply grieve the loss of the person you loved and shared multiple memories with, and also notice that the grief takes on a different texture when you realize that your loved one's journey is not over; it is just beginning on another plane. You can feel your sorrow and also allow yourself moments of deep peace (or maybe even a little joy) when you think about the soul's freedom and where and how that light will continue.

    I have had my own experiences with loss, death, and grief and have held space for countless clients who experienced the death of a loved one. I have shared intimate moments with those grieving in my office over the death of a child, the loss of a parent, or facing their own death when given a terminal illness. While discussing death can be a difficult conversation, being with your grief and sharing it with others can allow the healing to begin.

Many of us were given the messages as children to "Stop crying, or I will give you something to cry about," or "Big boys (or girls) don't cry." We learned to stuff our sadness. In America, we live in a society that often represses the expression of grief. The message is, "Don't cry at work you'll look weak," and "Don't show your emotions in public, you'll make others uncomfortable." But I wonder how humanity would heal more quickly if we were allowed to wail in the streets and publicly express our sadness without shame or embarrassment.

The traditions of the "death wail," which allowed people to cry their grief aloud, have been documented among the ancient Celts. They exist today among various indigenous peoples of Africa, South America, Asia, and Australia. Lakota tribe elders use the phrase "mitakuye oyasin" meaning "we are all related." The death of anyone in the tribe is felt by all. In many Native American tribes and cultures, death is not seen as an endpoint but rather as "walking on," which is the continuation of the journey. During mourning, grief is expressed through wailing, singing, crying, and cutting of one's hair or body.

Grief has been experienced so often in solitude and behind closed doors as people in our culture feel that sharing their grief will be a burden to others. What if like the Lakota, we embraced the grief experience and allowed it to be a shared experience with those around us, with the awareness that we are all connected? We are all a part of the same family of humanity and interdependent beings that are intrinsically woven together. We need one another and in times of grieving we can grow through grief as we embrace our sadness and allow others into the circle of our grief to support and hold us through the process.

The Mexican holiday, El Dia de los Muertos (Day of the Dead) is celebrated as family members remember, honor, and celebrate their dead relatives. It is believed that during this two-day celebration, the border between the spirit world and the real world dissolves and the dead are reawakened during this time to sing, dance, and celebrate with their loved ones. It is filled with beautiful traditions, symbols, and imagery. Incense, flowers, candles, and food line the altars and graves of the beloved that have passed. This is not a somber holiday. Instead, it honors the dead with festivities filled with color, music, and food honoring and keeping alive the memory of a loved one. It is believed that the spirits of loved ones come back during Dia de los Muertos and connect with the living. It is interesting to see how grief is transformed through these rituals. When grief is shared, and the dead celebrated, how does that transform our pain?

HEALING THE GRIEF

In my life experience and over three decades of working with others as they deal with and heal through their pain, there are some essential elements that are deeply helpful in the healing process. The first of these is being able to allow yourself to feel whatever you are feeling as you are feeling it. There will be moments of gutting sorrow, joy in remembrance, and at times even a sense of disorientation or disbelief. All of that is normal. Allowing yourself to feel what is there moment by moment by moment is what will allow you to move through it and truly heal. There is no specific time limit and no, "one size fits all," with grief. The timeline of your grief journey is uniquely your own. Other people might get scared by your grief and want you to "just get over it and move on," out of their inability to deal with their own feelings around grief. No one can dictate the duration, depth, or details of your journey but you.

And remember, you are not your grief. You are experiencing it. It will subside. You will have moments of happiness and even joy as you are going through it if you allow it. Often people tell me that they feel guilty because they experienced relief in the passing of a loved one who may have had a long struggle with a terminal illness. There is relief that the person's spirit is free and they are released from their pain or suffering. This felt sense of relief is normal and human and absolutely okay. If you were the caretaker for someone who was going through a painful or slow death process it can be absolutely exhausting, totally consuming, and completely overwhelming both mentally and emotionally. Of course there is relief when the pain has passed for everyone involved. Embrace yourself and the experience you are having. We are heartbroken when someone passes because we loved them and we feel it in our hearts. Thank God! It is evidence that the love we felt is still alive within us. Part of our human experience can be going to the depth of sorrow. Again, it is okay. I promise it won't take up permanent residence there. Just allow yourself to go through your own process, feeling and loving your way through it all.

Journaling what you are going through and giving voice to your pain is very helpful, as is sharing your pain with others. An emotionally safe place is essential where you can trust others to stay with you through difficult emotions, where you feel honored, respected, and cared for. As you are first going through your own journey, it is also absolutely appropriate and necessary to need your own time alone to process your feelings internally as well.

Again, you get to decide what serves you best. And if you aren't sure what you need, reach out and talk to someone about your feelings. Connection is a powerful healer.

THE IMPORTANCE OF CONNECTION

Connection is vital to who we are. It is also vital as we are going through the grief process. Neuroscientist Matthew D. Lieberman tells us, "Long before there were any primates with a neocortex, mammals split off from other vertebrates and evolved the capacity to feel social pains and pleasures, forever linking our well-being to our social connectedness. Infants embody this deep need to stay connected, but it is present through our entire lives." We inherently need one another. We are interconnected beings.

We know that social connection can lower anxiety, decrease depression, help regulate emotions, lead to higher self-esteem and wellbeing, and even improve our immune systems. During a time of loss, this becomes even more essential. At times in grief it might feel like you need to reach in before you reach out and that is ok. Grief is on your timeline. If a loved one is dying or you are aware of your own terminal illness, talking about this experience, discussing your fears, and planning what you want to happen after your death will actually help lessen the pain. Whether it is your legal will, your funeral details, or the celebration of life ceremony you or your loved ones would like to have, discussing this with your family and closest friends can help lessen the fear for everyone.

As a psychotherapist, I have worked with many people who have gotten the news that they had a terminal illness. When this occurs, there are many emotions that can come up. Fear, anger, deep sadness, and interestingly, sometimes, relief and surrender.

I worked with a wonderful man who found out he had three to five years to live due to a heart condition. Working through the difficult emotions, we were also able to talk about what was truly meaningful to him in his life, what were his golden moments and things he had treasured during his life journey, and how he wanted to enjoy the time he had left. We brought his wife into our sessions with us so she could talk about her fears and they could further enhance the communication between the two of them so they could enjoy the precious time left they had together. They talked about the importance of even doing the small things together, going out for ice cream, playing Scrabble together, or enjoying a good meal. Bringing conscious intention to how they connected, spent time together, and sharing what each of them needed as they went through this journey were important parts of the conversation. The love and tenderness between them grew as the fear lessened and this allowed them the room to create more meaningful times together in the present.

Think about the times you have spoken with someone about something you had been holding in or were at first afraid to talk about and then after sharing it experienced empathy, compassion, and understanding from them (and a sense of relief for yourself.) Remember how it made you feel to be seen, heard, and validated. This is one of the powerful reasons why we need one another as we go through life and especially through times of grief. We can only see ourselves or experience ourselves so far. We can validate ourselves all day long, but somehow, being witnessed by someone else and held in that energy of compassion and attunement, we are transformed.

SACRED LIFE

When I was a little girl, I had one of these life changing moments sitting by the beaver ponds up at our ranch in the Western Slope in Colorado. I started fishing those ponds with my father when I was four years old, wearing my red rain boots and my yellow parka. I have a visceral memory of the smell of sage, and earth, and the way the sunlight would reflect on the pond. I can hear the aspen leaves quaking, remember the feeling of a slight breeze on my face, and re-experience the deepest sense of contentment I held in my heart. There was nothing else in those moments other than the moment itself and that was all that was needed.

I felt deeply connected to it all, which is why by twelve years old I told my father I could no longer fish anymore. That last time I held a fishing pole in my hands, it was late in the afternoon and the sun was just beginning to move into the skyline, when I reeled in my last fish. The brilliant oranges, maroons, and deep yellows were already kissing the sky and reflecting on the water of the pond. It was as if time held in its breath and we were held there in that moment, timeless.

It was just my father and I casting at the water's edge. I can smell the soggy grass that was beneath my feet, and the whirring sound of my reel as I made that last cast. When the lure hit the water, something landed in my soul. It was such a beautiful evening, how could I take a fish from its beautiful home in this majestic setting? How could I rob it from its friends, its family, everything it had ever known? Just then the whirring sound of my reel and the sharp bend in my pole told me I had one on the line. Out of years of conditioned response fishing with my father, I jerked the pole back to anchor the hook, and began spinning the handle to reel her in.

When I pulled the fish from the water, I snapped back to my previous thoughts. "Dad! I don't want to kill it!" I cried, huge sobs choking from my lips. "I want to put her back."

"Ok, sweetheart, let me see what I can do," Dad said as he grabbed the fish, looking for where the hook was lodged." "Oh, I am so sorry love," he looked back at me, "It has swallowed the hook and I can't get it out without killing it." I remember the thud of the fish as Dad hit its head against the rock to end its misery. I wept and wept and wept. Huge sobs wracked my body as we walked hand in hand across the long grass of the field, away from the paradise of the pond and back into the waiting cabin.

We sat by the fire that night while the tears poured out of me. My father allowed me to grieve the death of that precious life and held me while I cried. He allowed me to make my own decision that I would no longer participate in causing death to the beautiful fish that swam in the ponds, because it was what mattered to me. I didn't have to stuff my feelings. I could share them and own my own experience of loss that was different from his. That moment changed my life.

At the tender age of twelve, I was profoundly aware of the sacredness of life and death. I was able to deeply grieve the loss of that fish, and I was also able to feel my intimate and deep connection with the pond, the sky, the trees, the water, and all the fish that swam underneath. I knew in the fiber of my being, that we were connected in a way that was beyond space and time and circumstance. Even if I didn't have the words for it then, I could feel how all of life, death, and our connection to it all, were all woven together in the divine and eternal tapestry of life. What started out to be a simple fishing trip with my father, turned into a vital, life-changing experience that helped me to understand how death, grief, and connection are essential elements in the continued circle of our lives.

EMPOWERED ENDINGS

I have had the joy of interviewing and being in further conversations with conscious entrepreneur, Elizabeth Uslander, the co-founder and spiritual director of Empowered Endings. She, along with her husband, Dr. Bob Uslander, has developed a phenomenal program to catalyze social paradigm shifts in End of Life Care. Elizabeth and her husband help others approach end-of-life care from every angle- physically, mentally, emotionally, socially, and spiritually. Building deep connections and rapport, they support individuals, their families, and their health providers, to support, guide, teach, and transform the experience of loss.

Elizabeth has held a lot of hands and has guided a lot of hearts through this process. When you meet her you feel this depth of soul from someone who has helped so many others navigate through the unknown waters of death. She has gleaned deep wisdom from her own life experiences with loss, grief, and death and has had an incredible spiritual journey throughout her life that has created a powerful alchemy within her as a death doula. Just as a birth doula ushers one through life, a death doula helps the soul transition back to the infinite.

Elizabeth talked about the importance of understanding your own relationship with life as you navigate through death and the importance of understanding what is in alignment with your spirit. In speaking about the grief journey she said, "Healing is really about connecting. It is through this connection that we can transform grief and the deep pain we are feeling, and this can lead us to authenticity and healing." She talked about how grief is a master medicine and it requires connection to walk through. If you allow yourself to be with the pain it will connect you to your deeper self. Resisting or running away only prolongs the feelings of pain and allows it to further embed in your body at a cellular level.

There is deep healing in connecting to others as you go through your grief journey. It is when you think you need to hide your pain or do it in the darker recesses of your room that you compound it. Bringing these conversations out into the light and getting support for you or your loved ones brings greater healing for everyone. Elizabeth shared that it is the heart-to-heart conversations she had shared with individuals and their loved ones that have helped facilitate powerful and peaceful transitions at life's end. She said, "We fear death because we don't know what "the end" is going to look like." Peace begins when you move away from having to know an "ultimate answer" and embrace that no matter what it "looks like" you are not alone.

"The most important thing is to be willing to feel—whether healing from grief, trauma, or crisis," She shared, "It can be hard and scary, and it can hurt a lot, maybe too much sometimes...so we tend to resist or avoid it." Elizabeth calls this the "Spectrum of Escape." While it might be normal to want to avoid pain, it will take longer to get to the other side of the pain and into the possibility of healing the longer you resist the pain that is there.

Elizabeth has a transformational process she's outlined to help people wrap their heads around the journey, giving them something concrete to focus on as they walk together in healing. She's found that the intensity of grief, trauma, and crisis can be challenging to confront or grapple with, so she created a simple, gentle process by which people can take "one bite-sized step at a time." She shared, "This lets them focus on something at which they can succeed, which encourages further development. It weaves a wide variety of traditions and practices together to support any evolution, ie: spiritual transformation, executive coaching, grief and trauma healing and so much more."

This is Elizabeth's creation and with her permission, I share it with you here. It is such a beautiful process and so essential as we befriend our own grief/death journeys and heal through the experiences of losing those we love.

Awaken: Recognize who you are, where you are, and what you're experiencing. Really connect with yourself in the moment, no matter what that means, looks like, or feels like. This often includes recognizing how your past has shaped and influenced you into becoming the person you are in the moment and how you relate to yourself and the world around you.

Embrace: Commit to fully embracing yourself in the moment, no matter how messy or painful it is. This is usually a long process, as it's deeply challenging to fully love and accept yourself, especially when you're just beginning the process or practice of doing so. Simply put, it's a life-long commitment to self-love, grace, and acceptance.

Envision: Imagine who you want to be, how you want to live. Connect with your future self, see yourself handling the same circumstances differently and achieving different outcomes. As you recognize the differences between who you are / have been and who you envision yourself to be, explore the different attitudes and actions that you may wish to change in order to become the new version of yourself. In alignment with Embrace, it's important to give yourself grace if / when you discover you can't or can't yet achieve a way of being or desired outcome—it may or may not be possible, today or another day. This is a visualization practice to connect with your Higher Self, your True Self, your Authentic Self, etc. depending on the individual's framework.

Release: As you identify the beliefs and behaviors that aren't aligned with your vision, you start to release those which do not serve you. An analogy she likes to use is: Your psyche is the garden, and you are the master gardener—it's your job to take care of the delicate flowers; to appreciate the giant, strong trees, and pull the weeds. Release speaks to the pulling of weeds, letting go of past habits, ways of being, ideas about who you are, or who you can / should be. The more we let go of who we are not, the easier it is to be our authentic selves.

Nourish: The opposite of Release, this is about identifying the beliefs and behaviors that do serve you well, and are in alignment with your vision of / for yourself. Using the same analogy of the garden, this is about tilling and fertilizing the soil, planting seeds, watering them as they grow, ensuring they have sunlight to thrive, etc. It's about getting clear on what works / what's effective in achieving your authenticity, and goals, and supporting yourself in those choices so you can consistently make more of them.

Surrender: Ultimately, this is what it's all about. The process helps your mind wrap itself around something concrete it can "do" while life continues to be what it "is." It's a process to help you more easily accept who you are in the giant web of life, relate to life on life's terms, and support yourself in living freely, authentically, and joyfully. This is the part where you trust the foundation you've built, giving yourself permission to meet life as it comes and trusting yourself to handle it authentically and in alignment with your values and vision.

The power of these five ways to engage the end-of-life grief process is stunning. When you embrace who you are and how you are moment by moment, you begin to create peace in your being. When you embrace the present moment as it is, you stop the resistance that says, "I am not accepting this moment because it is not what I want it to be." What if the process towards death was actually a process for you to know, love, and accept yourself at an even deeper level? And, you don't have to wait to be at the end of life to start engaging in this transformative process. You can begin right now.

YOUR OWN CONNECTION

When you are ready and the timing is right for you, you can experience connection to a loved one that has passed. This might not be in the initial stages of grief for you, or it might be something that you choose to do earlier, as it brings you comfort and connection to the loved one you have lost. Whenever it feels right to you, this can be a profound exercise to help you more deeply connect with your loved one in the current moment. I would invite you to have a journal handy for this process so you can record your experience, intuitions, and any insights that come through.

Find a comfortable place to sit down, bring your hands to your heart and take a deep breath into your heart space. Spend a few moments centering on your heart, and feel the expansion of your chest, just rising and falling with your breath. Imagine a warm sun gently pouring over your head warming your face, neck, back, shoulders, and streaming through your body. Breathe that sunlight into your heart and feel it radiating from your center.

When you are ready, allow yourself to float back in your mind to a pleasant memory with your loved one. As you tap into the memory you can allow yourself to go more deeply by focusing for a few moments on each one of your senses. Focus first on your sense of sight. You might see them smiling, laughing, and interacting with you. What do you see in the landscape of that space?

Go through all of the senses, continuing with your sense of sound. What did you hear in that memory? Hear your loved one's voice and hear the noises around you in the memory, both close up and further away. Were there any fragrances in the air? What did you smell? Breathe it all in. Was there a certain taste that you connect to that memory? Remember the food or beverage you may have been enjoying connected to that time. Allow yourself to marinate on the memory of it. Then move into your body. What textures do you remember feeling? What was the temperature? Notice if you were standing, sitting, or lying down and feel what you were touching in that memory or what was touching you. Really feel through your sense of touch into the memory and just notice your experience. Then breathe into your heart space and notice the emotions that are there for you. Let yourself feel the love and the joy that connected you to this person and to this beautiful memory. Let the wonderful emotions of the moment fill your being and breathe into them more deeply.

Feel your heart to heart connection with your loved one. Allow it to fill your heart space, transcending time and distance to experience a sense of "nowness" in the moment. Now expand that awareness back to you in current space and time, sitting where you are in the current moment. Feel into the top of your head and imagine that energy going up until it connects with your higher self or your experience of the Divine and then bring that light down to meet you inside of your own being. Allow it to radiate throughout your entire body. Let it be a soothing balm to any of the places that need it.

Then feel into the soles of your feet and imagine deep roots coming from them connecting you all the way down to the center of the earth so you are being held in perfect balance, anchored in the moment.

Then focus once again, breathing into your heart, and again hold the image of your loved one. What might they be saying to you right now if they could speak to you? Try not to "think" of what they might say, allow yourself to just listen to the answer that appears in your heart. Feel into the warmth that is the beautiful light of your loved one and know that they are with you now. Feel yourself embracing your loved one in the warmth of your love for them and then pause to notice what comes back to you. Just allow yourself to marinate in the love and the sense of connection until you are ready to end the session.

When you feel complete, rub your hands quickly and vigorously together (as if you were trying to start a fire between your palms) and then, with your eyes still closed, let the back of your hands rest softly on your knees, palms up, and just allow yourself to receive. When you are ready, and only when you are ready, slowly open your eyes. Write down anything that feels important and savor the feeling of connection.

CONTINUED HEALING

When someone you love dies, it can be a time of huge self reflection and an opportunity to truly evaluate how you are living your life in alignment with your highest self. It is a time when you can ask yourself, "How am I embodying the divinity that is within me?" Death brings you face to face with your essential self and your authenticity. Have you lived your life the way you have wanted to? Death's invitation to you during times of loss is to look at how you want to live more fully.

How well do you know the "You" beneath the surface; the eternal you? As you take this inner inventory it is an opportunity to purge what doesn't serve you, looking at what is truly important and meaningful in your life. It is like pruning the branches of a tree. Some limbs block the light so the tree can't thrive as easily. When you prune away the things in your life that don't serve you, and don't hold meaning to you, you are creating space for more life, vitality, and love to shine through.

You can gain wisdom as you reflect on the loss of your loved one and look at what their life lessons were and the lessons you gleaned from them that were passed on to you. Both positive and negative lessons learned can go through the alchemical process of becoming wisdom. Part of the beauty of being in a relationship with your loved ones is that their purpose and lessons in your life don't stop once they leave this earth, it may actually just be the beginning.

Ask yourself, "How am I showing myself love, tenderness, compassion, and understanding?" Perhaps this is an opportunity to increase your relationship with yourself. At times when you lose someone, it can feel like you are losing yourself. Keep anchoring to the spirit of your being. Meditate on your connection to the Divine, call in the lost parts of yourself through music, chanting, prayer, or song. Walk in nature and feel your connection to the birds, the trees, the sky, and the sun. Pause and breathe it all into your heart and feel your interconnectedness to all of life. Then, when you are ready, reach out and share your experience with those trusted people you love so you can also be held by that connection as well. If you need more help, reach out to a therapist or counselor who can help guide you through the process and help you to heal. You don't have to wait until you are in a grief process to dive into this deeper connection with your soul. You can start in this moment.

Elizabeth Lesser, bestselling author and the co-founder of Omega Institute, an education and retreat center focusing on health, wellness, and spirituality, offers this, "You don't have to wait for a life-or-death situation to clean up the relationships that matter to you, to offer the marrow of your soul and to seek it in another. We can all do this. We can be like a new kind of first responder, like the one to take the first courageous step toward the other, and to do something or try to do something other than rejection or attack. We can do this with our siblings and our mates and our friends and our colleagues. We can do this with the disconnection and the discord all around us. We can do this for the soul of the world."

TAPPING IN:

1. Write down the messages you were given about grief as a child. Was it ok to express your feelings? What was the appropriate expression of grief in your family of origin? What beliefs do you still hold onto today that you would like to release?

2. What in you still needs to be grieved? Remembering that your grief journey is unique, what needs to be further released (to make room for more peace and joy) and are you willing to allow yourself to do that? You might process this by yourself or utilize a therapist who can hold space and help guide you while you do this important healing work.

3. You are not alone in your grief. Connect. Connect. Connect. Allow yourself to reach out beyond your grief to let others support and comfort you. You can tell them directly what you need, and what might not be as helpful. You may need someone just to sit with you and not speak at all. Maybe just their healing presence is enough. You may want to talk out your feelings with a trusted source. That is fine too. Connect inside with your heart and ask it what it needs and then connect with what support you need on the outside too. Write a list of what you feel like you need each morning. It's ok if it changes day to day or even moment to moment. It is the check in and connection with your own heart that is the key.

Chapter Seven: Remembering the Past

> "It is perfectly certain that the soul is
> immortal and imperishable, and our souls
> will actually exist in another world."
> –SOCRATES

Life after life is something written about in most religious traditions. They all point to there being something beyond the veil of this life's experience. If we started having more conversations about the possibility of this being a reality and took it out of any religious or dogmatic debate, think about the powerful conversations we could have talking about the common thread of the shared divinity of our souls continuing on? When you think about your precious life being the graduate course into the next level of your soul's evolution, there is a realization that we are all in the same school and in this, our life experiences become even more precious. The lessons on how to express more love, show compassion, handle conflict, surrender, and find peace within ourselves and one another become paramount. Each is a lesson in how to allow the fullness of your authentic essence to shine through the container of the body you are living in. The evolution of your soul depends on your willingness to stay "awake" in class for the lessons.

According to a Pew Research Center report, many Americans say not just their faith, but other faiths can lead to eternal life. In a 2023 survey, 56% of people who believe that many religions can lead to eternal salvation also believe that people without religious faith can achieve eternal salvation as well. A similar number (30%) say that belief is the key factor in achieving everlasting life. Many religions, including Christianity, Islam, and Hinduism, believe in the eternal life of the soul. What if they are all pointing to the same thing and are just different paths to the everlasting life that is available for us all.

There is a growing number of people who are expanding their consciousness to a place that goes beyond religion or dogma, to the essence of the soul where we all have access to the eternal. There are thousands and thousands of accounts of people having near death experiences or having contact from the other side that makes them believers in life after life no matter what their religious background or faith tradition may be.

Millions of people, including myself, have had these "glimpses behind the curtain." It can be something that leaves a deep and lingering impact when you experience going to a new place and have the overwhelming feeling, "I have been here before," or upon waking up realize "Whoa! That was so vivid and felt too real to have just been a dream." You may have had some of these experiences yourself. We live in a culture that makes it more difficult for people to share these experiences because no one wants to be embarrassed, or ridiculed, or marginalized. Imagine what it would feel like to just honor your experience and have the social safety to share it because it was a part of everyday common conversation.

Think of your own experiences. Have you ever met someone and instantly felt like you had known them before, and so comfortable that the immediate connection you felt is hard to explain? Maybe you have traveled someplace for the first time and had a distinct and undeniable feeling like you already knew the place? Or woken up from a dream where the details were so crisp and the experience so visceral that it felt like it was all real? You can write this all off as "coincidences" or "just a dream," but maybe there is more to it. Perhaps in these moments, we are able to peer into our other lives and get a glimpse of our eternal souls in action.

I can only speak from my own experiences when I say that I have had dreams that were too vivid and emotionally felt too real to be "just a dream." I have had dreams that were so distinct in texture and tone, I knew during and afterward that I was experiencing something different than just a daydream or visualizing something. These distinct dreams are more like memories that feel like they live within my bones and are held within the fibers of my being.

My first experience of this happened when I was around six years old. I was watching a television show with my parents that took place in Europe. At one point in the show, a police car was chasing another car down the street. When I heard the sound of the police sirens, which are very different sounding from our police sirens here in America, I froze. The sound took me back to a vivid memory. I knew I had experienced this memory before, like a vivid dream, and it was completely clear to me. I could remember myself lying on the floor of the backseat of a car. I could smell the dust of the floorboards and the carpet that covered them. I could feel the rough wool blanket had been thrown over me to hide me. I could hear those foreign police sirens outside of the car while I laid in terror underneath the blanket. I peeked out from under it to see a police car going by while raindrops streamed down the windows. The person driving the car was a man who was trying to save my life. He looked back and said, "Stay down." That was it. Just this small glimpse. But the vision is as crystal clear and visceral today as it was at that moment 50 years ago. I still get the chills and have a strong reaction when I hear those kinds of European sirens on a movie screen. It feels far beyond coincidence and something I can't just explain away because I feel that memory in my being.

There are two other times I have had these "breakthrough" memories as dreams. As a young woman in my thirties, I dreamed that I was dressed in plain gauze clothing with a sash around my waist. It was hot and I noticed the dry, hot feel of the place I was in. Two men held me roughly by the arms and were dragging me down to a shallow river to drown me. Although I tried to pull away, they were so much bigger and stronger than me. I could feel their hands around my arms and the anger within them. I wasn't sure what I had done. I just knew I was going to meet my death. I had the feeling that I was someone who spoke out and told the truth about things they were trying to keep quiet, and for this, I was being killed.

They dragged me into the river filled with reeds and long grass and held my head under the water. I felt the struggle of swallowing water and water filling my nose and lungs. And then, peace. I suddenly felt my spirit begin to leave my body and I knew I was drowning. I felt like I could hear what the two men were saying to one another above the water's surface. One of them told the other to put his head below the water to see if I had quit breathing. As he looked under the water to make sure I was dead, I reentered my body fully, just for the last moment of that life that I had in me, because I wanted to scare him. I opened my eyes and stared at him. I could see the shock on his face and terror in his widely opened eyes. I could hear the scream that came out of his mouth in huge bubbles as he rushed up to the surface for air. It was my final act of defiance in that life. I woke up with a start and experienced a deep knowingness that I had just witnessed my own death in another life. It was far beyond "just a dream."

I have had many vivid dreams before this and since, but none that carried this internal message for me. For a long time I have only shared these with a few people because these are conversations most of us keep quiet, but it is time we share our stories. I have met thousands of people on my life's journey and have heard these stories from so many of them. So many that I have become deeply convinced that this is not an individual experience, but a collective one. I know at my core that we are given these glimpses beyond the veil; a shared knowing that this life for us continues on eternally, if we choose to listen and open our hearts to this reality. Our souls continue to evolve, and as we learn the essential lessons, we are able to heal and transcend. As we focus on and experience our own healing and expand our consciousness, we can help contribute to other's healing and increase the level of consciousness on the planet.

My third experience came ironically, during a session I was doing with my finance coach. Heather was helping me to break through limiting beliefs around finances and heal my relationship with money. It was wonderful and powerful work. It was during our last session that she guided me into a deep meditation and visualization. Its purpose was to tap into any past life memories that might be in the way of abundance in this life. Although this at first may have sounded, "far out there," I was willing to be completely open minded and cooperative with the process. We began with a relaxation and moved into the visualization. At one point in the visualization, Heather asked me to cross this high bridge and as I came down the other side, to see myself move into my past life experience and see what I noticed.

In my mind's eye, as I came down the other side of the bridge, I had the feeling I was in medieval times. I saw a gorgeous woman in a white flowing gown, embroidered with gold, and a handsome bearded man at her side. It was clear they were royalty. I felt so excited that this beautiful woman could be me in a past life! And then, the vision continued from the couple, and I felt myself going behind the eyes of an old woman that I recognized as myself. A haggard and spiteful old woman in a nun's habit. Through her eyes I was seeing the beautiful couple and I was critical of them flaunting their wealth and was jealous of their youth and stature. I had pledged a life to God and poverty and so envied the life of these two such fortunate beings. I could feel my loneliness and the deep sadness I carried within me. I knew I wasn't a privileged person and because of my birth into a certain caste, I would remain poor without the ability to change my station in that lifetime.

It was all very powerful. I was aware that I had in some ways carried this poverty mentality within me. Even though I have been very successful in my career, the message has always been, "I just have enough to make it." This felt like an important awareness and a turning point in a more abundant mindset.

Now here's where it gets interesting. What happened next is one of those things we have talked about where you find yourself saying, "You just can't make this sh*t up!" I had a Zoom call with my meditation teacher Elle planned for a couple of hours after my session with Heather. I was on a deep healing path and these two sessions just happened to land on the same day. In my work with Elle, we would go into wherever I was feeling; sadness, fear, or other shadow emotions and just meditate on and explore those spaces. Sometimes these meditations would last for hours.

On this particular day, as we moved through the meditation, I felt a great healing light and energy come over me and through me in a powerful way. I felt the presence of someone guiding me on this inner path and being beside me as I went through this process. There was an inner alchemy that felt as if it was rearranging my energy and cells, creating greater wellbeing within me. When we wrapped up the meditation practice, Elle asked me, "How was it?" I said, "Incredible! I feel so light and my body feels amazing, like I have really let go of something deep and important." "You did incredible work," she shared, "I could really feel the energy moving through you." "But I just have to tell you," she added, "The most interesting thing happening during your session was the nun sitting at your feet the entire time."

MANY MEMORIES

In his book, *Many Lives, Many Masters, The True Story of a Prominent Psychiatrist, His Young Patient, and the Past Life Therapy that Changed Both Their Lives*, Brian Wiess explores the idea of past lives and reincarnation. If you haven't read it, this book will change your life and paradigm around life, love, parenting, relationships, being a spiritual seeker, and life after life. Brian is a graduate of Columbia University and received his medical degree from Yale University. He had been a traditional psychotherapist until he met Catherine who came to see him for treatment.

Catherine had been having recurring nightmares and anxiety attacks which still continued eighteen months into intensive psychotherapy treatment. Although she was very motivated to do well, was a good patient and capable of insight, she was not healing. Catherine had been afraid and had resisted hypnosis but finally agreed to it. Hypnosis can be extremely helpful in reducing anxiety and eliminating phobias and negative behaviors. In hypnosis, through focused concentration, the body can relax and the memory is sharpened. Some people are able to remember early childhood events in this calm state of being.

Catherine began to recall details of her past lives while under hypnosis and received messages from spiritual beings known as the "Masters." Although Brian had been a natural skeptic at first, through his sessions with Cathrine, the veil was lifted and Brian began to believe that the spiritual "Masters" were providing help from beyond. These Masters offered insights to the mysteries of the soul, the purpose of life, the afterlife, and evolution.

Through recalling her many lifetimes and receiving messages from, "the space between lives," Catherine was able to share specific and accurate messages from Brian's family and his dead son which there was no way she could have known. The wisdom that was transmitted through Catherine through their amazing work together, cured her anxiety and negative symptoms and became a spiritual awakening for Brian. This incredible experience they went through together during these powerful sessions changed them both profoundly. Not only did it diminished his own fear of death, Brian became more intuitive, compassionate, and humanistic. By the end of the book, you witness Brian moving from skeptic to wholehearted spiritual practitioner. The messages in this book are powerful, speaking about the souls progression through love and wisdom, harmony and balance, toward a mystical and ecstatic connection with God.

STEVE'S STORY

One of my dear friends shared with me his recent experience of regressive hypnotherapy. He did a specific type called Quantum Healing Hypnosis Therapy and the experience for him was profound. He has been on a beautiful spiritual path and this experience opened up whole new worlds to him.

Steve shared that he remembered three specific lifetimes. When he dropped into these memories, he said the smells, the textures, and what he could see and touch, were all vivid and visceral. In the first life, Steve saw himself living in a small village where he had a very quiet life. He shared that the life lesson for him was about communication and harmonious existence with nature. At a very deep level, he understood that we are meant to listen to nature and to only participate when nature speaks first and that all things are provided to us by nature.

He then was shown a memory of another life where he was a clergyman in a church in Italy where he was in a ceremony helping to heal a person that was in the center of a circle surrounded by he and other healers. Steve knew that this lifetime for him was about service and devotion. He felt he was born into this life very devoted and dedicated so he could learn the art of self discipline and ego surrender, which have been things he has strived for in his current lifetime. At one point in the visualization, he saw his own death. He said he was aware that he was dying but it was full of much peace and ease, feeling he had lived a good life.

The third memory was that of being a military person. He viscerally tapped into being an angry jet fighter in his final moments before his plane went down. He felt it must have been in Vietnam or WWII and he experienced himself as an Asian pilot. Steve said he was filled with rage as the plane was going down. He realized that the war he was fighting was not his own. As his plane began to crash into the ocean that would be his death, his final vow to himself was, "I will never fight someone else's war." Steve said it was powerful as the plane was crashing into the ocean, he became aware of the fear he had in his current life of heights and the feelings of claustrophobia that he could never make sense of until that moment in the visualization.

When I asked him how this experience informed his life now moving forward, Steve said, "I now have a deep knowing in my body. There are aspects of myself and tools within me that I can now tap into." He shared that he felt supported by this knowingness and that these memories he experienced in past lives are now reference points that he can lean into.

Steve felt a depth of connection with his soul's lineage. He said, "Even if none of it is real, I feel I have more understanding, deeper wisdom, and can trust myself more." "We are in a Master class," he shared. "Regardless of how naive someone may seem, everyone's soul is here for the Master class."

THE WITNESSING

Bestselling Author, Professional Psychic, Reiki Master Teacher, and Energy Healer, Lisa Campion and I had an extraordinary conversation about her phenomenal experiences with life, death, and the afterlife. Lisa is one of these beautiful and rare people who was born psychic. We are all born psychic she says, but Lisa came out of the womb already aware of this. Her twin brother had died in utero at fourteen weeks gestation. His soul remained connected to Lisa and she became aware that his soul contract with her was to keep in contact so she would be able to better share her psychic gifts to help others.

Her very first memory of being alive was that of being a little baby in her crib and having these radiant light beings surrounding her, smiling and blowing kisses until her mother came into the room to check on her and then they all disappeared. As a little girl, Lisa had dead people showing up in her room, but stated that she was never afraid of them. She realized that they were just spontaneously stepping from one place to another and she was able to witness their life/death/life cycles. She also could see the green lush paradise portal that people passed through and came back from so she said was never afraid of death. Lisa understood it as just the "doorway" that souls kept going in and out of, just like someone would move from room to room.

We spoke about what happens when someone dies and their soul has a lot that is still unresolved. Lisa shared that sometimes people get stuck. She used to experience these people as a child and would call them the "gray people." These souls were sad, lonely, and lost. They couldn't resolve something during their lives and were stuck in a trauma loop in death. Much like what might be described as kind of a purgatory, they could not ascend or go to the light. Lisa, as a medium, helps people get unstuck by creating the bridge through conversation and connection with them that helps them to resolve their trauma and forgive themselves and others. In what she calls, "The Witnessing," Lisa witnesses their trauma and validates what they had gone through. She says to them, "Just look up. You have to surrender. You can go to the light. You are already forgiven."

Lisa shared that once a soul crosses over, they are able to see things from a different perspective so the relationships that couldn't be healed in life, can be healed from the other side. She said, "The soul is able to see their part in it and is no longer clinging to or connected to their ego self. As soon as the person dies, they are starting to let go of their egos. They release self attachments and are already going back to their higher selves." The process has to do with releasing false beliefs. "When we are alive, we really believe that our thoughts are true." She said, "Sometimes it takes dying to find out that they aren't true at all."

When I asked Lisa about her own past life memories, she shared that she has always had a strong desire to travel and that our souls have an affinity for certain places that we may have lived in other lifetimes. One of the most profound experiences she shared with me was her memory of when she was in France in 1985 and was studying abroad her junior year in college. She shared about the time she was with a tour group that went to Aix-En-Provence to the Senanque Abbey. The Abbey had housed a Cistercian group of monks that had lived very hardcore lives and had adopted very depraved practices as a way of going against the lavish Catholic church. Practices included having to walk for a mile to get a sip of water, having very little food, and even depravity in their living quarters with no glass in the windows to keep them warm.

Lisa remembers it being very glum and having very dark energy. While she and the tour group were in the main sanctuary, Lisa suddenly got a very strong urge to cross the rope that kept people from accessing the rest of the monastery. Something internal took control as she crossed over the rope and moved through the monastery, knowing its corridors intimately. She made a beeline directly to a monk's cell that she immediately knew had been her own. Lisa knew she had lived there as a young monk in his twenties for the short time of eighteen months and had then died of starvation and pneumonia. She began to sob uncontrollably and ran from the cell, again knowing exactly where she was going and ended up at the Abbey's cemetery. Lisa went straight to her own grave from that lifetime and threw herself on it, sobbing hysterically.

"When I left and went back to the group, I felt healed afterwards," she said. "I picked up a part of myself that I had lost during the trauma in that lifetime." Lisa feels throughout her life she has traveled to places where she has continued to find these lost parts of herself and heal them. In a vision quest in her thirties, she experienced lifetime after lifetime of the moment of her deaths. Some were more peaceful and some were horrific. She commented, "Death itself doesn't hurt, it's the pain and suffering we have on the way that hurts. If we can remind ourselves that we are going to feel so much better once we are out of this body, we can relax into the relief and comfort of death as the end of pain and suffering."

This is so profound. "Death itself doesn't hurt." That is the release, the grand awakening into a higher realm of being where the pain of this physical body doesn't follow you. No one likes to feel pain. When you become aware that the pain of this life is temporary and that your soul is eternal, you can begin to quit fighting the resistance to the pain which is actually what causes your suffering. Emotional and physical pain happen to us. Suffering is a choice. Death is the release from all of the pain and suffering. When Lisa shared about the pain she endured at some of the final moments of her life, it was excruciating, but in a flash, it was over and the bliss and the higher self that were immediately experienced beyond death removed any trace of the previous pain.

It's like the amnesia we as mothers have felt when we have given birth. We don't remember the pain or we would most likely never get pregnant again. But something beautiful happens and the pain fades away and as we are holding that baby, we are in an altered, higher state of being. In birth as in death, we are taken to the higher realms of our spirit.

YOUR SOUL CONTINUES

Even if you have never had a past life experience or have never had the feeling that you knew someone before, you can still find peace in knowing that so many millions of people have. Just like 50,000,000 Elvis fans can't be wrong, these shared experiences speak of a deeper truth that can't be ignored. There is something more here than what meets our earthly eyes. Pay attention to your dreams and your knowing beyond reason. This is the essential time to trust your inner G.P.S. that will guide you beyond the conditioning of your mind to the eternal truth of your soul. It is imperative that you tune in and that you learn how to trust the Divine that resides inside of you and that connects you to the whole.

Ask the Divine to help you tap into the timeless through dreams. Release any clinging to having to have the answers and see what shows up. Begin to open up the essential conversations with others and be open to what they have experienced and if you have experiences of past lives yourself, find people you can be safe sharing them with. I promise you won't have to search far. These stories of life after life and people that have experienced them are EVERYWHERE.

TAPPING IN:

1. Have you ever had a profound moment of deja vu or times when you have met someone and you had such an instant connection that you felt like you knew them before? Make an inventory of these events and people in your life. It might have happened more often than you realized before.

2. Even if you do not believe in reincarnation, just notice if you have a certain draw towards a certain culture or location on earth. Notice when you are in a new place you have never been to before, if you start to recognize the streets and buildings and seem to know your way around. Pay attention when you get that sense of recognition as you experience people, places, or things and start writing down and keeping track of these occurrences.

3. Try something new. Hypno Regressive Therapy, float tanks, shamanic work, sound healing, deep meditation, and breath work are a few of the modalities that can help you access a deeper connection to your soul. Think about what might work best for you to keep excavating that light that is inside of you and allow yourself to tap into the possibility that your light has always been and will forever continue. If you do receive some information from your intuition, the Divine, or even from a past life memory, utilize it to inform, create, and design a better life for yourself currently.

Chapter Eight:
Essential Interviews

> "If you have knowledge,
> let others light their candles in it."
> –MARGARET FULLER

Over the past six years, I have been deeply honored and profoundly blessed to have had interviews and conversations with some of the most brilliant minds and serving hearts on the planet. Through my roles as a filmmaker, retreat leader, and as a radio show and podcast host, I have had the phenomenal opportunity to absorb and extract the distilled wisdom of hundreds of remarkable thought leaders and changemakers in our world. I have sat in the heart of the deepest and most meaningful conversations of my life with these beautiful souls. The topics of love, peace, awakening, consciousness, spirituality, and life and death have informed my own experiences and expanded my understanding of our connection to the eternal. I felt it essential to share some of the golden nuggets from those conversations with you.

Emily Thiroux Threatt - *Author, Podcaster, Speaker, and founder of the Grief and Happiness Alliance*

In my beautiful conversation with Emily, she shared with me her personal stories of loss in the deaths of her two husbands.

One died in 2006 and one in 2017. Her first husband was sick two years before he died and they had discussed his imminent death at length. Emily shared, "You think you are prepared for something like that, but you're not." She shared that she was lost after his death and spent a lot of time by herself. She never dreamed she would get married again but then met her second husband, Ron. They had a wonderful and positive relationship. She said he truly taught her the joy and happiness that came from living in the present moment. Emily felt so blessed that she had two wonderful husbands in her lifetime to love.

When Ron got ill they moved to Maui. When he passed, Emily found herself feeling isolated from the mainland, but knew she wanted to stay in all of the beauty that Maui offered. She continued healing and a part of that healing has been from the connection she has still experienced with Ron. She shared a memory of when she and Ron were dating and the time he said to her, "I heard this song today and this is our song." She said, "Okay." although she said she didn't know the song. Ron was able to find the words for her and as she read it thought, "Oh, yeah. This really is our song." It was a song by Stevie Wonder. She said it was your ordinary run-of-the-mill song, but as life went on, the song kept coming into play at different times in their lives.

Emily and Ron had one good friend who moved to Maui when they moved there. The friend ended up living with them at their cottage and became an important and beautiful part of their lives as she helped take care of Ron while he was sick and dying. This friend knew the story of their song. Only a few weeks before my interview with Emily, she shared she had just had an extraordinary thing happen.

Emily shared that she had been at an event that her good friend had put on that had a live band. She said they were both just sitting there enjoying the music when the singer addressed her friend and said, "There is a song that I have always wanted to sing for you and I just never had the chance to sing it before, but I want to sing it today, and it is a Stevie Wonder song." Emily's friend looked at her and said, "If that song is "As" we'll know that Ron is here. Emily thought there was a slim to none chance that it would be that song but how cool it would be if it was. And then the band started playing; "As." Emily said it was absolutely fabulous and as the band knocked the song out of the park, she and her friend sat there and wept through the whole thing. The singer didn't know the connection Emily had to the song, but for Emily and her friend, the connection was clear and Ron was right there with them.

Steve Farrell - *Evolutionary Pioneer, Author, Global Speaker, and Executive Director and co-founder of Humanity's Team*

I felt such a heart-level resonance when I spoke to Steve about life, consciousness, and his new book, *A New Universal Dream.* Upon meeting Steve, I was struck by his deep wisdom, incredible kindness, and serving heart. There were so many peak moments and incredibly invaluable insights shared in this interview, I had to distill it down to share some of the most precious gems here.

Steve spoke about how we are designed as part of "The One" and how science and quantum physics are backing this up. He said, "The new universal dream is our whole universe (the Divine) and the fact that we are all inseparable from it, just like waves are inseparable from the ocean." Steve shared that what we realize is that we are one with the stars, the earth, and with nature, all in beautiful harmony. We are intrinsically connected to all of that and our basis is that harmony, peace, and love. Steve added, "Instead of walking around in what Einstein called an 'optical delusion' where we have the illusion we are separate from one another, at a quantum level everything is deeply connected, interrelated, and interdependent where we are all one."

Steve also shared that when we begin conscious living, it begins with our own journey and personal transformation. As we transform, there is a spillover effect and we extend it out to others. When we reach this tipping point, we are aware of the divine presence in ourselves and within others. He said "It is where you are seeing the interior of this person in front of you as a sacred person with everlasting life and unlimited potential. We still see the physical beauty of that person that we see today, but the spiritual beauty, the sacredness that we see as well, creates a whole other experience."

Having worked with some of the most powerful psychics, mediums, and people that have had near death experiences, Steve talked about how they are all saying that we have this beautiful potential to lift the veil to pure light and pure love as we go through that tunnel of light to the other side. Steve said, "As we lean into that awareness we realize that it is all pure light, and pure love. And that this "separate thing" as we transition (into death) just melts away." He discussed how in our transition, we realize we are all a part of each other and all a part of the divine as our basis. We are all part of the infinite and divine circle of life. When we awaken to our infinite soul we can live, as Steve says, "the delicious life" of service and connection with one another in new and profound ways.

In his essential message at the end of the show, Steve shared, "What is said, that we all read and paid attention to in Sunday school for two minutes, is that we are all made in the likeness and image of God. That is true. It's not something to understand for two minutes, it's something to really understand. You were sent here on this planet, at this moment when we are in the middle of the greatest shift of the ages that has ever occurred on this planet." He added, "Please don't let this be a little two minute thing that you just put down, please allow yourself to really know that and live into that, that you are the son and daughter of the most high." What a huge effect this would have on ourselves and our world if we lived into this truth.

I think it is so powerful when you realize that you are a powerful being and a powerful creator on this planet and that you can have an important impact on the world if you want to. When you begin the practices of self compassion, sensing your connection with others, and conscious living, you will begin to heal yourself and add to the healing of the planet. As we each continue this practice, the consciousness of the world evolves. Awareness of our infinite nature and as powerful co-creators with the divine can open up a whole new way of living in harmony, love, and peace in the world. The potential of this possibility excites me to my core.

Arielle Ford - *Celebrated love and relationship expert, best selling author, international speaker, and leading personality in the personal growth and the contemporary spiritual movement*

Firey and fun, I always love talking with Arielle Ford. From my past interviews with her, I knew she was not afraid of death, and had actually learned in a Nadi reading in India, the exact age she would be when she died and how it would happen. When I spoke to her about this in a recent conversation she shared that she actually felt very excited about dying and that she couldn't wait to see everyone. She exclaimed, "I want a day trip to heaven! Not through drugs or a near death experience, but actually just going there for a day!" Arielle said she knew that her sister Debbie, who had passed, would meet her at the gate and would show her around. She said, "It would be like having an "E-Ticket" into heaven for the day."

When asked about what her experience has been with Debbie since her death, Arielle said, "Debbie comes to me in dreams and she is absolutely beautiful! Her skin is so luminescent that I am saying in the dream to myself, 'I have to get my phone and get a picture of this!' and I say to myself, "Oh my God, this is real!" Not only does Debbie come to her in dreams, but also directly through communicating with Arielle in her mind. In one example, Arielle shared that her sister came to her and said three times, "Tell Kim to go for it!" Arielle hadn't spoken to their mutual friend Kim in years, but upon the insistence of her sister, she called Kim.

"I am supposed to tell you," Arielle began, "That Debbie sent me a message for you and I have no idea why." She told Kim the message and Kim immediately lit up. "I know exactly what she means! Thank you!" Eight weeks later, Kim called Arielle back to let her know that at fifty two years old, she was pregnant. She and her husband had been debating having a child together at her age, and they were really on the fence, but Debbie's message was just what she needed to hear to make the decision. With a donor's egg and her husband's sperm, a precious embryo was implanted and Kim gave birth to a beautiful, healthy, little girl who was carried to full term.

Of course Arielle deeply grieved the loss of her sister. She shared how important it is for other people to know how to be with people who are grieving. "When I was grieving, the most annoying thing people kept asking me was how I was feeling. How the f*ck do you think I am feeling?!" "It is a no-win situation," she said. What would be more useful, Arielle said, would have been if someone would have asked her, "Is there anything you could use or want?" or "Would you be open to me sharing one of my favorite stories about your sister." When the right questions are asked during grief it makes all the difference between further upsetting someone or truly comforting them.

Arielle shared a story from her childhood when she first made peace with death. At seven years old, she remembers waking up in the middle of the night and her grandfather (who wasn't visiting and wasn't living with them) was sitting at the end of the bed. She said she and her grandpa were both favorites of each other and they shared a really special relationship. Her grandpa told her that he was going to go away but that he would always be connected with her.

Arielle said that her grandpa disappeared and then the phone rang immediately afterward. She heard her mother scream and then her dad came into the room and told her her grandfather had just died. "Yes, I know," She said, "He came and told me."

Today, Arielle lives her life without regrets. She says from her years on this earth she has learned that the times that seemed like the most horrible moments in her life, eventually turned into something unexpected and wonderful and they turned out to be the best thing ever. Both her life and her relationship to death are stunning examples of what happens when we fully embrace, and relish the fullness of it all.

Mark Nepo - *Philosopher, teacher, best selling author, and spiritual teacher chosen as one of OWN's SuperSoul 100, a group of inspired leaders using their gifts and voices to elevate humanity*

In my heart resonant conversation with the wonderful Mark Nepo, he shared powerful tools for dealing with the fear around death. Not everyone may be aware of the fact that Mark almost died in his 30s from a rare form of lymphoma. Now in his 70's, Mark recalled how he started to grow a large tumor on his skull while he was a university professor. He felt healthy other than the tumor but it continued to grow until it was the size of a half a grapefruit. This went on for three months until it miraculously disappeared. Mark felt he had truly experienced a miracle until a sister tumor showed up and started growing on his rib.

He shared that he wasn't afraid of death when the first tumor appeared, but when the second one showed up, he became very afraid. The rib and the tumor were removed and Mark started a very aggressive form of chemotherapy. At three and a half months into treatment, the chemo started to kill him, so he had to stop. He said he has been healing ever since.

This experience took Mark to a point in his life which he describes as, "A more naked and authentic place." He said he was challenged to believe in everything from all of the spiritual traditions. "Because of this, all of my teachings and all of my books have a commitment to the unnamable common center of all paths," he shared. Mark said it is the poet in him that "sees," the philosopher in him who "tries to understand," but that it is the cancer survivor in him that says, "Ok. How do we make use of this? Where does this fit in our daily lives?" That is what informs how he lives, teaches and is in community with others.

I asked Mark about the gift in sharing our stories and bringing our fear out into the light, not hiding it inside of us. He talked about fear being like a virus. He said, "Although fear has its place in alerting us to danger, legitimate danger, by being human we inflate and deflate our sense of ourselves and our situations all the time. We are always challenged to "right size" our fear." Mark talked about the importance of acknowledging our fear, but to go deeper to ask our souls what to do when we are feeling the fear.

He said fear held in the chest keeps it going, but by letting it go and expressing it, it's not so heavy and it doesn't make so much noise within us. The most powerful thing we can do is admit that we feel it. When we admit our fear and when we keep each other company through it, the fear can be transformed.

"Right now we are being asked to become intimate with the unknown," Mark said. "We don't have a lot of practice with that because the modern world has trained us to think of the unknown as only bringing us catastrophe, but the unknown also brings us wonder, and joy, and surprise. We are being asked to expand and animate our relationship with the unknown."

During his cancer journey, Mark said he had a powerful experience that changed his life in beautiful ways. He had studied the ancient Chinese poet, Du Fu across time and stated he was the one person Mark had wished he could travel back across time to meet. Mark admitted that he was terrified at this point dealing with his cancer treatment and his fear of death. One night, during this time, Du Fu appeared to him as a guide in his dream. Mark said in this particular dream, Du Fu was sitting cross legged on a beach and was holding a stick that he was just moving in the sand. Mark went up to him and said, "How do I block the fear?" Du Fu ignored him and Mark got irritated and angry and got closer to him and again said, "How do I block the fear?!" And without looking at Mark, Du Fu raised the branch above his head and said, "How does a tree block the wind?" and with that, he disappeared. Mark woke up with the instant thought, "Of course a tree doesn't block the wind. It lets it through." And that was his first deep lesson about fear. You can't block fear. You have to let it through.

As you allow yourself to face your fear around death, you allow more light to enter it. You can see the fear as it is. Your fear is heightened by focusing on the past and/or the future. Neither of which you have any control over. But you can, as Mark says, "right size" your fear when you breathe into the moment and let the light that is always available to you to come through. When you allow yourself to show up as authentically as you can in this moment, express and release your fear, you loosen fear's grip and power over you. When you allow yourself to be connected to others through this process, and allow them to truly see you and hear your fears, you transform the fear into connectedness and the light of healing begins to flow through you.

Mark said, "We are not just isolated and alone…We are connected to everything. The reward for being authentic and living life as fully, honestly, and tenderly as possible, is that we are joined by the rest of life…When we don't hold back, we can experience this oneness with others."

You are not alone. Reach in and then reach out. Share your feelings and your fears with others and be like the branch of a tree in the wind, and let your fear flow through you. The other side of that is connection, light, happiness, and a deeper sense of connection to your true self and the oneness of all that is.

Neale Donald Walsch - *Beloved author (33 titles in the last 20 years, including the Conversations with God books, which have been translated into 37 languages and read by millions), international speaker, and modern-day spiritual messenger*

I could not write this book without including Neale Donald Walsch. Not only was our conversation the catalyst for this book, he has been a spiritual guide and mentor to me through his books and films for the last twenty years of my life as well. Before our interview on my podcast, we had such a heart-to-heart connection and such a beautiful conversation that we could not even get to the recorded interview for half an hour. At one point during this conversation, Neale paused, looked at me and said, "Stephanie, you are going to write a new book. You are going to start this new book tomorrow, it will have a global reach, and I will write an endorsement for this book." Needless to say, the next morning, I began to write the book that is now in your hands. When I receive Divine guidance, I answer the call.

Our conversation and the interview that followed were life changing for me in many ways. I found a kindred spirit in Neale and felt his deep wisdom speak straight to my heart. Neale shared about a time when he was face to face with the potential of his own death. In 2007, he found out that he was going to need open heart surgery. Not a double bypass, or a triple bypass, or even a quadruple bypass, but a quintuple bypass. At first, he said his mind wanted to say, "This was the worst news," and certainly everyone else was saying that. But quickly he moved to, "It's what is. It's what's happening." He said he allowed himself to embrace the moment as an opportunity, "To announce and declare, express and fulfill, become and experience," who he really was.

As he was being wheeled into the operating room, the doctor paused to allow his wife to be with him for a few minutes before the surgery. She exclaimed "You seem incredibly peaceful and calm about all of this." Neale said, "Darling, only one of two things can happen. Either I die and go straight to heaven or I recover and go straight to heaven when I come home to you." He shared that he wasn't even trying to be romantic, it was just the truth of how he was feeling. Neale told her, "Being with you is heaven and going to heaven is heaven, so you know what? I am in a no lose situation."

Neale didn't resist the fear of death, he just looked at the reality of it. "What you resist persists and what you look at disappears," he told me. When Neale woke up from the surgery, the doctor told him the surgery had been a success and that Neale had just bought himself ten more years of life. That was almost 20 years ago.

We had such a beautiful conversation and I invite you to

listen to it in its entirety on my *Igniting the Spark* podcast. It is one of those rare opportunities when you get to listen in and learn from a master. One of the most powerful things Neale shared with me during our conversation was the question he had asked God, "What is the most important message you want me to hold in my heart?" And God replied to him, "Sweetheart, it is very simple. Your life is not about you. Your life is about everyone's life you touch and the way in which you touch it. And when you live your life in that way, you will step into a larger reality, a universal truth that at a cosmic level your life really is about you - for one elegant reason - There is only one of us in the room."

Marcelene Dyer - *American author, narrator, meditator, and speaker, wife of the late Wayne Dyer*

You know when you first meet someone and you just have a deep sense you have known them before? That was the experience that both Marcelene and I shared the day we got on the phone together. I felt like I was talking with an old friend and we were just catching up and could easily and naturally share the contents of our hearts, as close friends do.

Marcelene shared about her life as a little girl in Pennsylvania. From a very young age, she carried a deep peace within her that lasted throughout the challenges of her life. From three years old, she would walk daily with her five-year-old brother and mother across St. Joseph's cemetery which was a shortcut from their house to the grocery store and to school. She remembers how sacred that land was and how she would walk with reverence through the cemetery, as to not step on a grave. Even in the winter, she said, she made sure she knew where the graves were. She would study the tombstones, these gateway markers to the eternal, and felt that death transformed her.

From infancy Marcelene went to church. When her mother stopped going, she still went with her father and when he stopped going, she went by herself. She fell in love with the tenets and the hymns sung in the congregation. The church called to her. There was something beautiful and deep within her seeking truth. She explored all religions around her town looking for answers from them to save her from dying, and instead, she was taught how to live gracefully.

She had a "love list" that she prayed for each night that included family, friends, and even the mailman and paper boy. Then she would plug her ears and wait for what she now knows was Anahata Nada and she would stay with her ears plugged listening to it until the sound ended. The Anahata Nada is from the spiritual teachings in ancient India. It refers to a mystical and profound auditory experience, unlike any typical sound we encounter in daily life. This phenomenon transcends the usual auditory experiences, entering the realm of deep spiritual experiences and insights. Clearly, Marcelene was in touch with a deep spirituality far beyond her chronological years.

We spoke about her relationship with Wayne, how they met, the love and connection they shared, and the amazing children they brought into the world. Marcelene shared that at forty, she and Wayne met Deepak Chopra and stayed at his institute for a week where he taught them Transcendental Meditation and it was there she realized she had been doing it her whole life. When Deepak gave her a mantra, it took her practice to new levels where she started to awaken to visions and seeing deities.

At her home with seven children, she said she had a sign she would hang outside of her bedroom door while she did her twenty-minute meditations which said, "Mom's meditating. Unless you are bleeding to death, please don't disturb me." Marcelene stayed at home with the children while Wayne toured. She lived happily and with passion, being present with her family. She remembers the living room covered with toys and things the children could play on and someone coming over and asking, "Do you run a daycare?" and she just laughed and said, "Yeah, I guess I do!"

Marcelene's fifth child was her daughter Serena. She said from the very beginning of Serena's life things were different with her. Serena was always crying and had to be carried around in a sling, connected to her at all times. At two, she would stare at her hands and rock back and forth. Marcelene and Wayne were preparing themselves for how she may or may not develop. And then it suddenly stopped. Things became even more interesting when Serena started to speak and would say, "You are not my mother. I didn't live in a world like this. I lived somewhere before."

Eventually, Wayne and Marcelene went and saw Lynn Web who is a famous medium in Seattle who channels Lee Chang. She told them that Serena was a child of Vietnam in her last life and that she didn't want to be born. Her father had been killed in battle and her mother and brother had died, so Serena would wander from village to village alone looking for food.

This all rang true for Marcelne because, at their home, Serena continually hid food around her room and on her person. Because they lived in Florida and Marcelene was afraid of getting cockroaches, she said she worked out a way for Serena to keep having her little bits of hidden food, but to keep it in plastic baggies. Serena also would speak in her sleep in a dialect that Wayne lovingly teased her about, calling it her, "wing ding ling ching" because it most definitely sounded Asian.

At twelve years old, Serena wanted to go to a network chiropractor with her parents. A network chiropractor uses evidence-based approaches to healing, wellness, and body awareness.

Greater self-awareness and conscious awakening of the relationships between the body, mind, emotion, and expression of the human spirit are realized through this work. As Serena started working with the Chiropractor, she began rocking and sobbing and sobbing. The doctor said Serena had a breakthrough that could take adults fifty sessions to achieve.

Serena asked to talk with Marcelene afterward and told her, "I saw my whole life backward. My family died and I was buried alive." Although Marcelene had never been taught reincarnation through her religious upbringing, she knew this was true. She and Wayne began to remind Serena that she had chosen a life of safety and security as a continued affirmation until eventually, Serena had completely healed from the trauma of her past life.

Marcelene has survived the death of her husband Wayne and her daughter Sommer, who both have come to her in visions, dreams, and through signs. Their relationships both living and in the afterlife have been profound teachers to them all. The veil between worlds has dropped for her, and she lives in daily sacred connection with all of her children on all sides of the veil.

Throughout her 73 years, Marcelene shared that God has been her best friend and that in this LOVE she exists. Through the tools of love, prayer, and meditation, she experiences peace and sees that as the awakening on earth is happening, the results of those tools are a kind-filled, peaceful goodness for everyone. As the birth mother of seven children and eighteen grandchildren, she experiences each one of them and each day as a gift. Marcelene is a gift to us all.

Stephen Simon - *film producer, director, and production executive, co-founder of Spiritual Cinema Circle, and producer of the Academy Award® winning film What Dreams May Come (starring Robin Williams and Cuba Gooding Jr.)*

You know when you meet certain people and there is distinct light emanating from them? That has been my experience every time I talk with Stephen Simon. In our conversations, he beautifully shared with me the amazing journey he has been on with his wife Lauren who has transitioned to the other side.

From the moment Stephen and Lauren met, they realized they were both very deeply, spiritual beings. They weren't tied to a particular religion but to a deep spirituality that informed them both that this lifetime is our human life, and that our souls and consciousness live on. This is something that quantum physics is now proving.

They had many conversations about what would happen when one of them passed and they discussed and designed what they wanted their afterlife to look like and be like. They both believed in the powerful adage, "When you believe it, you will see it." Lauren and Stephen decided whoever passed first would find a way to connect with the other. They knew they were twin flames that had been together many lifetimes and were deeply connected by the powerful love they shared. Like in two of the films Stephen produced, *Somewhere in Time* and *What Dreams May Come*, the message is clear: "Love lasts forever."

Stephen said that they both thought he would be the first to go because he was seventeen years older than Lauren. On January 3, 2018, Lauren, the love of Stephen's life, suddenly passed away in her sleep, at the age of 54. When Stephen found her that morning, he went into total shock, grief, and PTSD. He called one of his dearest friends, Neale Donald Walsch, who drove the four hours from Ashland to Portland, Oregon, to be with him for the next 24 hours. Two weeks later, Stephen called Neale again and was crying inconsolably saying, "I am out of my mind with grief!" Neale said to him, "Good Stephen, you need to be out of your mind and into your heart."

The six weeks after Lauren's death, were excruciating times for Stephen. He was so heartbroken, he said he felt like a stranger in a strange land. At times, he begged God to take him as well, so he could be with her. After six weeks, Lauren connected with Stephen from the other side. He said it was in a way he absolutely knew it was her. Stephen was watching a television series episode and was about to turn off the T.V. because he didn't want to see the credits and the preview of what was coming next (something that he and Lauren had always avoided when she was alive and watching a series together because they didn't want to spoil the surprise of the next episode.) Stephen felt a very distinct voice in his heart. He shared it was important to note that this did not come from his head, but that it was a felt sense in his heart. Lauren said to him, "Honey, watch the end credits." "What?!!" Stephen thought. "We *never* do that!"

He and Lauren both knew the importance of things coming from the heart. "The brain is a mini computer that files everything you experience in life and then spits it back. The mind does not understand the everlasting life of our souls, but our hearts understand," Stephen shared. He agreed, "OK. I'll watch it." Stephen said he kind of fell apart because as he watched the credits, a song he and Lauren loved was playing, "Ooh, child things are going to get easier, things'll get brighter…We'll walk in the rays of a beautiful sun…When your head is much lighter," the beautiful lyrics rang out. Stephen knew it was her saying, "Honey, I love you, I'm with you, and I will be with you until you're back over here with me." And that began their adventure together over six years ago that continues to this day.

Stephen shared that Lauren connects with him almost every day. When Lauren wants Stephen to know she is there, Stephen says there is a very specific "tell." For Stephen, there is a physical change in the density of the air and a very personal and private way between the two of them that tells Stephen that Lauren is with him. He said it is different for everyone. Stephen laughed, "It is beyond magical because we are talking like we always did. It's us making fun of me like we always did." The beautiful relationship and the depths that they shared continue.

Lauren began to explain to Stephen more about the other side, what happens when we transition, and told him about what the contract was that he and she had made with each other. Stephen began taking notes on yellow legal pads because he knew he wouldn't be able to remember everything from their conversations. Stephen continued to write things down from his meetings with Lauren for several months. She told him about how we create our reality on the other side. Stephen remembered a line from *What Dreams May Come* when Robin Williams first meets Cuba Gooding on the other side and Cuba says to him, "We all paint our own surroundings here. You're the first one to use real paint!" If you haven't seen the film, it is a must see. It is a powerful film and a phenomenal scene.

Several months later, Stephen went to Ashland, Oregon to visit one of his and Lauren's daughters. He said when he travels to Ashland, he always makes it a priority to see Neale as well. That night Stephen met Neale and his wonderful wife Em at a local restaurant they all loved. Now, it is important to note that Ashland had not seen any measurable rain in several months and was having quite a drought (a point that will be essential as this story continues.)

At some point, they started talking about what was going on with Stephen and his conversations with Lauren. He told Neale, "I've been taking these notes like you did in *Conversations With God*." (Because that's what Neale had done as he was taking notations from God on yellow pads as a diary for himself, never intending to write it as a book.) "I'm doing the same thing as you and as I'm compiling these pads, I'm getting the sense that this actually needs to be a book."

At that moment, a huge bolt of lightning flashed and lit up the room and a huge peel of thunder roared. Everyone was startled. Then Neale said to him, "Obviously, you need to write the book, and I know the title." Then another lightning flash! "You need to call it What Dreams *Have* Come." Then the lightning flashed again! Unbelievable! Stephen replied, "Oh my goodness, that sounds fantastic. And you know Neale, I'm beginning to feel like I need to write this with Lauren." Another lightning flash! Stephen said they were all sitting there enthralled because they knew they weren't in Kansas anymore! The rest of the evening was spent marveling at what the universe had just said, "Yeah, Dude! Get to it! This is what you need to do!"

When Stephen got home and could be quiet, Lauren let him know, "Honey, that was not me. I can't do that! But the universe did that to show you, "Yeah, we need to write this book together. So, let's get started!" And they did. From that point forward it took two years to fully complete their book. Stephen said the things that Lauren told him, he wrote down word for word in the book the best that he could remember them. In the book, *What Dreams Have Come,* all of Lauren's words are written in italics to denote her voice. He said so many people are having the same experiences out there so he and Lauren wrote the book so they would not feel alone. Such an amazing and beautiful outpouring of their love shared with us. Their love story continues to this day.

We discussed the miracles that had transpired in both of our lives about how more and more people are waking up to higher levels of consciousness. Stephen said, "Something is really going on in consciousness right now. Some quantum physicists are now saying that if Robert Oppenheimer was alive today, he would be working on some sort of device which could communicate between this life and beyond the veil." Stephen said he is just happy that he has his angel on the other side helping to show him the way.

What is the common message of these amazing people in the above interviews? They are giving you a grand invitation to experience a larger truth than you may have experienced before. They are giving you an opportunity to explore the contents of your soul for your own answers to the question of what happens when we die. And most hopefully, they are giving you comfort, like a soft blanket wrapped around you on a chilly day, to remind you that you are not alone in this journey and you are being held by a love that is more vast than you may have imagined.

TAPPING IN:

1. Let yourself journal the answers to these questions: How would you show up differently in your life if you knew you were intimately connected to the Divine? What would you want your conscious agreement to be with a loved one so you could connect when one of you is on the other side? What might be signs either one of you would want to receive so you could tap back in with one another?

2. Would you want to know the time and circumstances of your death if you could find out? What are the benefits for you of living in the mystery? If, like Arielle Ford you want more information about your life and your transition to the other side, go to: https://indianpalmleafreading.com/.

3. It is a powerful process to write down and share your own experiences. There are platforms and places you can share your experiences anonymously or you may choose to join a group so you can feel more validated in your experience. The most important thing is to believe in what you have experienced. You aren't crazy, although being in touch with the other realm can feel like something our mind struggles to grasp. Confide in trusted people and know that your stories matter. You may just be offering the validation that someone else desperately needs as you share your story.

4. To share your story with me, go to: YourBigFatJucyLife.org. You can choose to be anonymous, or you can share your name. Whatever feels best for you. These stories will always be kept confidential and will not be shared with anyone. I am here to listen, to understand, and to support you in your journey.

Chapter Nine: Connecting Past the Pain

> "A father holds his daughter's hand for a short while, but he holds her heart forever."
> **–UNKNOWN**

Life is full of relationships. Poor communication and difficult relationship dynamics may have kept you from having a healthy relationship with someone you love. Sometimes the only way you can heal your relationship with someone is after they are no longer on the physical plane. Sometimes, it is only through the death of that loved one that you can arrive at the more universal truth of what lies beyond personalities and problems and access what lives within the soul.

To say that my father and I had a complicated relationship is a complete understatement. I have shared with many people that my father was one of the greatest loves of my life, as well as one of the deepest wounds. I was born a daddy's girl and until the time he left our home, I spent every moment I could with him; playing catch in the side-yard (he used to tell me I would be the first female quarterback,) fishing on the Poudre River close to where we lived, faking I was tired so I could curl up next to him on the floor when he took naps on the weekends, and just hours and hours of me sitting on the floor of his office at home, coloring, or writing, or looking at the fish in his fish tank. I just wanted to be near him. When I was in his presence, I felt treasured and precious, and deeply, deeply loved.

It's funny how you remember the little sayings or moments from your childhood. When we drove together, and were looking for a certain place he would tell me, "Keep your eyes peeled!" I would excitedly scan the landscape and when I spotted it, he would enthusiastically say, "Good eyes, good eyes, Stephers!" I was filled with joy. My dad had asked something of me and I had helped him. Those small moments mattered to me. I felt valued, I felt important, and I felt seen.

This all dramatically changed when he left my mother. One night, in the winter of my thirteenth year, my father waited until he and my mother were snuggled in bed with the lights off to tell her he was in love with another woman and wanted a divorce. My younger brother and I were slumbering in our beds when the commotion broke out and our happy and carefree childhoods were completely shattered. No one, including my mother, could have seen this coming. My parents never fought in front of us. My mom and dad would laugh, and talk, and hug, and kiss in front of us. We ate dinner together every night as a family and we were constantly doing things together. Both of my parents were very involved in all of my brother's and my activities. The night my father told my mom he was leaving was as if a nuclear bomb had been dropped on the most beautiful landscape and all that remained were the ashes and the rubble of a treasured life once lived by all of us.

At thirteen years old, and being a daddy's girl, when my father moved out, I naturally went with him. I loved my mother, but she was emotionally struggling at the time, and I didn't have the internal skills yet to deal with it. What started out as a new beginning and special time with my father, quickly ended once we moved in with his girlfriend and her children (who were soon to become my new stepmother and step-siblings.)

She admitted to me years later that she felt like I was the "other woman" and that my dad loved me too much in a way that she felt wasn't healthy. Regardless of her reasoning, from the moment we moved in with her, until the day my father died, I was not allowed to be with him alone, I was not allowed to talk to him alone, or once I moved out, I was not allowed to talk to him alone on the phone without her being on the other line.

My father changed too. He told me that I was no longer #1 and that his love for me had changed. He became more distant and totally focused on their relationship and her needs. At that young and vulnerable age, all I could hear was that my father no longer loved me and that somehow, I had become unwanted and unlovable. I never wanted my father all for myself. I just wanted a normal father-daughter relationship with him like we had when I was growing up, ones that I continued to see with so many of my girlfriends and their fathers. I wanted that father I could go to for advice, the person I could lean on when times were tough. I needed someone who valued me and our relationship and the knowledge that it was okay to be treasured and loved because there was always enough love to go around for everyone. I just wanted to still be his, "Stephers," the little girl he had adored.

It got worse before it got better. At sixteen they wanted to move to Austin, Texas from the town in Colorado where I had grown up. By this point, my friends had become the most important thing in my world, and when asked if I wanted to move, I said I wanted to stay in Fort Collins with the friends I had known my entire life. After a huge argument, my father and stepmother moved to Austin and didn't speak to me for almost a year. I was gutted. Underneath it all, I still adored my father. I longed to be close to him and to be the little girl who ran into his arms after he returned home from a business trip. I longed to feel special, valued, and important, but instead, I felt I didn't matter.

During the next 32 years, I grieved the death of my father. He was still very much alive in the physical form, but the man who had been my beloved daddy as a young girl was gone. We saw each other on yearly vacations with his wife and the whole family, but we were never close again. It was a heartache I carried with me throughout my life.

THE WAY THINGS CHANGE

When I was 48 years old, my father had a heart attack and was in the hospital in a coma. He and my stepmother had been walking through the park on one of their daily walks when Dad had fallen to the ground. A dentist who knew CPR happened to be the next one on the trail to meet up with them and he administered CPR until the paramedics arrived. I was told Dad flatlined and they had to use the paddles of life on him to shock his heart back into action. He was then taken into a hyperbaric chamber and "frozen" because Dad had had a lack of oxygen to his brain. Research has proven that by doing this, more brain damage can be prevented.

For months, at the time, I had been working on the email I was going to send to my father and stepmother to tell them in the most loving and respectful way that I could that I no longer wanted to have a relationship with them. But when I heard the news of my father's heart attack and knew he was in ICU, I did not hesitate to book my flight. My brother and I both flew out to Austin within 24 hours of hearing what had happened. When we arrived at the hospital, we had already been warned by our stepmother that he hadn't woken up from his coma yet and to be prepared to see him hooked up to all sorts of machinery.

When we walked in the door, I saw him lying there so peacefully. I walked up to the edge of his bed and gazed lovingly at him and said, "Hi, Dad." And he opened his eyes. My stepmother gasped! "I knew he would open his eyes when he heard your voice. He has been calling for you in his sleep." These are perhaps the nicest words she has ever said to me. Permission and an acknowledgment that it was okay for me to matter to my father.

His progress and recovery were a very slow process. It was a full month before they were able to operate on his heart and perform the quadruple bypass that was needed to save my father's life. In those first few days we were there, once he had opened his eyes, he was in a very childlike state. He would open his eyes wide with wonder when he saw me and spoke in whispered tones, repeating three phrases, "You are beautiful," "You are precious," and "I love you." My father's essence, beyond his personality, beyond past experiences, and his mind's conditioning, was shining through. I knew beyond a shadow of a doubt that I was hearing the purity of my father's spirit, the one that is always connected to the Divine, is always connected to my heart, and is always connected to the love between us because that is what it is made of.

My father was in the hospital for two months, although my brother and I had to fly back to our lives and careers after being there for a week. After a third month in a rehab facility, he returned home and little by little, his old personality returned. The more disconnected, judgmental, critical father returned. It was heartbreaking really. It always seemed like there was something he disapproved of that I or my children were doing, and I again grew tired of phone calls from him and my stepmother that left me feeling devalued and less than.

After a year of trying and still feeling like I had to continually earn his love, and was still never good enough to earn it unconditionally, I sent the letter that ended our relationship. I never heard from or spoke to my father again while he was alive. I pressed the "send" button, and a thousand pounds were lifted off my shoulders. I never looked back or regretted that choice. I chose instead to continue my own healing journey. I focused on the gifts I had received from my father and the pure loving essence I had seen from him in the I.C.U.

Six years later, I received a phone call from my brother at 10:34 at night. I knew at that time of the evening; that it couldn't be good news. Earlier that year, my brother had shared with me that my stepmother had put my father in a nursing home after he had started to show signs of dementia. My brother told me my father had a stroke and was in the hospital again and he was flying out to see him, as the doctors thought Dad would not gain consciousness again.

And that was when the dreams began. For twelve nights in a row, every night I would dream of my father. The dreams didn't even feel that significant really. Some nights we would just be playing cribbage (a game he had taught me as a girl) and other nights we would just be laughing together or walking through the woods. I was aware of the deep sadness I was feeling knowing that my father was dying during waking hours, but in dream space, we were there together and it radiated pure joy throughout my very soul.

Two days before he passed away, my brother called me from his hotel room there in Austin with a confession. He said, "Steph, I don't know why I have never told you. But for the last six years, every time I talk with Dad he asks about you and how you're doing and says for me to tell you that he loves you." "What??!!" I shot back, "Are you kidding me?! Why wouldn't you tell me something like this? It could have been such a game-changer for us!"

He took a deep breath in. "I guess I just wanted to stay out of it and I felt like if Dad wanted to know how you were doing and wanted to tell you he loved you, he should just grow the balls to do it himself." I was crushed. I truly couldn't say if it would have made a difference in our relationship. I didn't have a crystal ball, but it was phenomenally important to me to know that even though we were no longer in connection during those years, my father had still loved me and cared about my wellbeing.

"Brother, please hold the phone up to his ear and let me tell him I love him," I requested. Even if he is unconscious, I know his soul will be able to hear me. "Steph, I can't do that." The night before, my stepmother had been furious that my brother had even told me that my father was in the hospital and my brother was afraid that if she walked in while he was holding the phone to my father's ear or found out I was speaking to him, there would be hell to pay.

I never got to say goodbye to him. I never got to tell him I loved him one last time while he was living. My opportunity to express to him that the little girl in me still loved and adored the daddy he had been, in this lifetime was gone. I sent him all the love I could muster up in my being and I held onto my heart's truth that my dad could feel my love within him. And then my dad, the greatest love and deepest pain of my life, was gone.

The dreams continued even after he passed. The rest of the world faded away and it was just me and my dad again, side by side. In dreamtime I remained his little co-pilot, forever, his little Stephers.

CHAPTER NINE: CONNECTING PAST THE PAIN

"I'M STILL HERE"

My father died on the 6th of December. A couple of days after his death, I was back at work in my office. I worked on the top floor of this beautiful old historic building in downtown Fort Collins. From where I sat in my therapy chair, I could see the withered vines that grew around the large picture window that my clients sat in front of on a blue-green, leather loveseat. That day as I was sitting with a client doing E.M.D.R., the largest bird I had ever seen swooped down into the alley and landed on the telephone pole (that I never even noticed was in that alley until that moment.)

At first, I thought it was an owl because it was so big, but as it perched there facing me, I realized it was a hawk. A huge hawk. I had never seen such a thing, especially in downtown Fort Collins. It didn't move. Minutes went by and the hawk just perched there looking at me through the window. I was flooded with the sense that my father's spirit had come to visit me through this majestic animal.

My client sat there with her eyes closed and I continued the session. After five minutes, I said, "Excuse me for a moment," and I took the phone that I was using as a timer for the 90-second E.M.D.R. sets and quickly snapped between sets and quickly snapped a picture of the bird. I thought, "No one is going to believe this." I was able to capture an image of this creature whose appearance somehow filled me with a deep comfort and a real sense of connection with my father.

A few days after the hawk incident, I was online looking for a personalized Christmas ornament for my boyfriend. When I clicked on Etsy and scrolled down the page, I was stunned by the ornament that appeared. The ornament that came up on that very first page was a large round wooden ornament that had a hawk in flight through the middle of it with the words underneath, "I will always be with you." Full body chills. Even now, as I write this, I have them again. That was just too huge of a coincidence to be a coincidence. My father's love for me was coming through beyond whatever had transpired between us, beyond my inability to tell him I loved him one last time, beyond any separation or sense of doubt that my father had loved me. He was sending me signs he was there, he was with me, and we would always be connected. I bought the ornament.

THE CONNECTION CONTINUES

Right after my father passed my boyfriend and I started to experience interesting things going on electronically in the house. Our brand-new dishwashing machine would suddenly turn on by itself, (it did this a few times that first week after dad passed, which it had never done before.) Our digital clock on our new oven would suddenly be at random times and the date on the clock would be switched to a different date. Again this had never happened before and it hasn't happened again after those first few weeks.

The wildest thing that happened is that I would get into my car, and the electric seat would be pushed all the way back. This happened three different times. The first time it happened, I thought to myself, "Why was my boyfriend driving my car?" At six one, if he drives my car he has to put the seat back. But later, when I asked him about it, he said, "I haven't been in your car." I knew this was true the next morning when it happened again. After returning the seat to its normal place, I got back into my car later that afternoon, and the seat was set back to accommodate a larger driver again, with my boyfriend nowhere around. "Okay, Dad. I said out loud, with a laugh, "I feel you."

CHAPTER NINE: CONNECTING PAST THE PAIN

Sometimes the volume of the car radio would randomly get really loud and I wouldn't be able to turn it down no matter how hard I tried to turn the dial. I just started saying, "Hello Dad," when these things would occur. As I write this I have full body chills, my inner truth meter is going off and I have soft tears in my eyes. For me, these signs were beyond a doubt, my father reassuring me his spirit was still there and his love for me, beyond the pain, distance, and separation, was still there enduring and everlasting.

I had the incredible Marla Frees on my radio show and podcast a couple of years before my father passed and we had shared a wonderful spark between us that continued afterward. Marla spent 25 years as a successful stage and television actress and was on my show sharing her life and discussing her new book, *American Psychic*. Marla was born with an amazing gift of psychic abilities. In 2006, she left the stage and screen to further pursue how she could help others with the gifts she has been given. She studied with the renowned James Von Prague for three years and has worked for decades with detectives in the L.A. area solving homicide cases that had gone cold. She currently has appeared as a psychic medium on A&E, Bravo, History Channel, SyFy, TV Land, and Gaia TV's "Beyond Belief" with George Noory. On YouTube, her video series with physicist and author Tom Campbell, blends physics with metaphysics to help others understand the "science" of how Marla works.

A couple of weeks after my dad passed, I had Marla back on my show. As we were having a wonderful conversation about what was happening in her life now, she suddenly paused. "You're dad is here," she said calmly. It is a moment caught on video that I will treasure forever. At minute 26, as Marla stated this, a bright orb of light came across the screen that anyone watching the video could clearly see. Marla laughed, "Did you see that?!" Full body chills. "I couldn't have missed it!" I exclaimed.

"Your dad has some cleanup work to do in the next couple of months, but he wants you to know he will come back and meet with you in the middle of February." I didn't know how to respond. I felt a thousand different feelings. Excited, in awe, sad, hopeful, blown away, and interestingly, very, very much alive. All of my senses felt heightened, I had a feeling of time slowing down and a sense of being held in that extended moment. Of course, despite the myriad of feelings I was experiencing, I ultimately said, "Yes!"

On February 16th, Marla and I met again, and she shared with me that she had been talking to my father for a couple of hours before our call. I had never experienced a medium before. The closest experience I had was when my sister-in-law died very unexpectedly from a staph infection in her early 40's. My brother-in-law, who was definitely a bit on the conservative side and would have considered a medium very "woo-woo," actually ended up going to one who was able to tell him some very direct messages from my sister-in-law, with exact details that he and she would have known about their lives and their home. My experience with Marla was very much the same.

She said my father was extremely sad and that he wanted to tell me he was so sorry that he had allowed his love for me to be filtered through his wife. He wanted me to know that he knew I loved him and that it was okay that I didn't get a chance to tell him when he was passing. He apologized for the wasted years when he was absent from our relationship and shared that he felt very sad about that. It was unmistakably my father coming through this call.

This last December, on the morning of the first anniversary of his death, I woke up with a profound peace within me. I had cried my eyes out the night before and had looked through old pictures of us when I was a little girl before he and my mother had divorced, and I was still his little co-pilot. I had sobbed deep gut-wrenching sobs thinking of all the time that had been wasted and how I had spent most of my life missing him and grieving the loss of my relationship with him long before he died. He came to me in dreams that night. I remember showing him different rooms in the house that I owned in the dream. I had worked on these rooms and was excited to show him what I had created. The next morning, I awoke feeling comforted and connected to him.

At lunch that day, I had to run to the grocery store to get treats for the Divine Inside Women's group I would be facilitating that evening. This is a group I created that meets in person the first Wednesday night of each month, to meditate, laugh, grow, and expand together. As I crossed the street to walk into the store, a profound sense of lightness came over me and I could feel my father's pride in me and the work I was doing in the world. I had a clear sense he was telling me that he was proud of me. As a psychotherapist himself, I felt him acknowledge that I was continuing his professional legacy of improving other's lives and helping them to heal. My heart smiled. I thanked him for his message and walked into the store with a deep sense of knowing that this connection to the best of him, was what lived on inside of me.

I still miss my dad. A part of me had been grieving the loss of him for the last 43 years since our relationship dramatically changed. When he passed away last year, I uncovered a new level of grief that I had not yet experienced. I cried for the little girl in me who had always waited for her daddy to come home after a long business trip so she could jump into his arms. I grieved the loss of the precious moments of childhood, where my father would read me a story each night before bed and then hold my hand until I fell asleep. With an aching heart I remembered the countless tag games he would play with me and my friends, and the sound of his laughter when we watched movies together. And I grieved for the unhealed parts within him. The parts he would never be able to heal in this lifetime and the dreams of his that were left unfulfilled.

What continues to soothe my soul is the connection I feel to my father now which is stronger in his death in many ways than it was during most of my life. Since his death, my father has continued to appear in cameos and as the main character in my dreams. Sometimes we are just talking, and I wake up not remembering the content of our conversation. Other times, I have profound moments in dream space with him and I wake up understanding something deeper about myself and my life. What I do know for sure, is that the relationship with my father never came to an end, it has merely taken on a different form. His love and the light of his essence, continue to shine and our relationship continues to heal throughout time.

TAPPING IN:

1. Have you had difficult or challenging relationships in your life that you weren't able to repair while the person was living? Take a moment to find a quiet place, find a pen and paper, and write a letter to the person that has passed that you were not able to heal your relationship with. Say all the things that you wished you would have said or didn't have the opportunity to share. When you are finished, put that letter aside, clear your mind, take a couple of deep breaths, and write yourself an intuitive letter back from that person. Just allow yourself to tap into the purity of their soul that resides on the other

side and see what comes back to you. Trust what you receive and let go of any feelings of regret for what may have been unspoken before.

2. Notice if there are any animals that represent your loved one that has passed and then notice how you feel when those animals appear in your life. Once the spirit is free, it can come back to you in many forms. When you continue to notice a certain animal showing up that represents a lost loved one, just send that animal pure love. It has been sent as a messenger from beyond.

3. Notice if you are still holding onto negative feelings connected to someone who has passed. Doing a release ritual will help you to let go of them. Buy a few flowers at the store. They don't have to be fancy or expensive. Just flowers you can easily pick the petals off of. You can go to a river, the park, or even to your backyard to perform the ritual. Sitting quietly, bring to mind that which you wish to let go of. It may be words, emotions, or memories that are no longer serving you that are connected to the person who has passed.

Take each petal off of the flowers one by one. As you do, hold each petal separately to your heart, and bring the intention of what you are letting go of from your heart into the petal, blessing it with love. If you are by a stream or river, you can put the petals in the river and watch them float away or you can release them into the wind. Close the ritual by bringing prayer hands to your heart and sit in the stillness of gratitude for the healing that has occurred.

Chapter Ten:
Into the Mystery

"Of course, you don't die. Nobody dies. Death doesn't exist. You only reach a new level of vision, a new realm of consciousness, a new unknown world."

–HENRY MILLER

COMING TO THE END

Interestingly, just like in life, this final chapter is not the end, but hopefully just the beginning of a deeper relationship you have developed with your life and with death. Perhaps now, death is not a prickly thorn bush that must be avoided at all cost because it is painful and piercing. Maybe it has become more of a gentle river, that floating upon the wisdom of shared stories, you can navigate with more skill and awareness.

Goodbyes can be painful. They are made more painful when you feel like they are forever farewells. It is perfectly normal to grieve deeply when a precious life here on earth ends. Knowing that death is one kind of ending, you may need to cry, wail, write, read, move, connect and share your pain as it best serves you. You most surely will miss the physicality of the person who has died when they are gone and are no longer able to hold your hand, or wrap their arms around you in a tender embrace. Missing, grieving, and honoring those losses are essential parts of feeling into the totality of your soul and are evidence of what happens when you truly love another. You will miss them when they are gone. And yet, when you are open to having a new kind of relationship with someone after they have transitioned to the other side, you have just opened yourself to a new depth and dimension of relationship that you could not have experienced before, one that you were not able to access in the same way while that person was living.

Death takes us through a purification process. As the personality and ego are stripped away, what remains is the stunning and pristine purity of the soul. To connect to this level of purity with a loved one is both a magnificent and transformative experience. You can have a relationship that you may not have been able to experience while that person was living. The love and relationship continue beyond death. When you set aside your doubts and drop into your heart, you are able to connect with the formless and timeless dimension that is the eternal sea we are all swimming in. Sometimes, we all need someone to throw us a little safety rope, a reassurance that we aren't swimming alone through unknown waters. As we begin to share our stories with one another we create a liferaft for us all to climb aboard.

That is the beauty of this experience we all share. There are groups everywhere where you can find a community to help consciously support you as you journey into new uncharted territories of connection beyond death. When you connect with others as you are exploring this new frontier of life after life, you will have your own experiences validated and will come to understand that what you may have written of as just a dream, or maybe your imagination getting the best of you, is actually a shared experience with millions of people all over the planet. The number of people reporting these experiences is growing every day. The veil is thinning and the information that is being shared on both sides will give you great comfort. You will see your loved ones again, your soul is going to continue, and the connection with those you have lost is available now. The message is extremely clear in both spirituality and in science, "We are never truly alone and death is never truly the end."

THE REVISITING

Just recently, I decided that I wanted to do something that would honor the essence of my father. I have kept his ashes in the box they arrived in almost two years ago now, in my meditation room. My father grew up on a Nebraska wheat farm with a huge windmill that adorned the property in front of the all brick farmhouse. It has been a special symbol to him that he continued to collect in pictures and sculptures throughout his life. At nineteen years old, my one and only oil painting I ever painted, was of a windmill for him, in the lush green, grassy fields of farmland. In my backyard I have a ten foot, small, steel windmill that is tucked in a corner of the yard among flowering bushes and a wall of green foliage and this felt like the perfect place to create something special for him.

I woke up early on that Saturday morning and dug a hole right by the windmill to plant the beautiful yellow, black eyed daisy mums I had purchased. I opened the black box Dad's ashes had come in; the one's with his full name and his birth date and death date on it. With reverence, I scooped a handful of my father's ashes into my hand, and breathed a deep breath into my heart, becoming present with the texture of the ashes in my hand. After praying over them, I scattered the ashes in the hole I had just dug into the fertile and waiting earth and placed the flowers on top. I gently put in the loose dirt until the flowers were nestled snugly in their new home and lit the candle I had brought with me. When I closed my eyes, the sunlight streamed through my closed lids, creating patterns of blue and yellow and purple and I felt the Divine presence within me. I paused here and let the light of the Divine shine in and through me and I felt the deep and loving connection I have to the pure essence of my father.

I placed a beautiful rock that has concentric circles radiating from its center, on the ground beside the flowers. That rock has traveled hundreds of miles and many years with me from the time when I had found it, twenty years ago. I had found it during the trip when my daughters had traveled back with my father, stepmother, and I to that magical ranch property that I had spent so much time at as a child. The rock had spoken to me and held significance as being the reminder of the happiest and purest memories of my childhood.

After placing the rock very intentionally on the ground, I continued to pray by the windmill. The pure essence of my father and his love for me radiated in my heart. The earth, that he was now a part of, would nourish these flowers that would bloom year after year in testament to the continuation of his soul. In honoring my father in this way, I had created sacred ground.

My brother arrived the next afternoon. He has not stayed with me alone for decades, but on this rare occasion, it was just the two of us. When he walked into the house, I could feel the presence of my father, feeling happy that my brother and I were together. I showed my brother the changes I had done in the house and the memory spot I had created for our dad.

Eventually we made our way to the gray couch in the front living room, and as we often do, fell into deep conversation, discussing all of the contents of our hearts with one another. As we were talking, all of the sudden the doorbell, which hasn't worked in years, began to ring. And super interestingly, it was just a solid, "ding" that droned on for about 10 seconds until my brother got up and went out and pushed the doorbell button again until it finally made a "dong" sound and was silent. No one else was there.

"Hi, Dad!" I said out loud and we both laughed. "That was wild!" We continued our conversation, laughing off what had just happened, until the lamp beside my brother began flickering for at least 30 seconds. "Whoa!" What's going on?" He asked. "I guess Dad just really wants us to know he's here," I responded. I had owned that lamp and its twin that sat on the end table on the other side of the couch for only a few months and neither one had ever flickered before.

The next morning when we woke up, with a warm cup of coffee nestled in our hands, my brother told me, "Steph, I had a dream about Dad last night. The first one I have had since he died and it was so real!" "Oh my gosh," I said excitedly, "Tell me about it!" My brother told me that in the dream it was exactly as my home looked now, and that our dad had entered the bedroom where my brother was staying and said to him, "I just wanted you to know that this is real, I'm okay and I am with you." My whole body shivered; truth bumps registering all the way through me.

"That reminds me of what Saje Dyer told me about what happened when she saw her dad in a dream after he had passed," I said. "He came to her apartment and everything looked just exactly as it was when she was awake." "Oh my god! I just remembered something!" He exclaimed. "There is more to the dream! But finish what you were saying about Saje."

"Well," I continued, "She said that he looked just like he did when he lived in Maui, and he told her it was all real and then he asked her to touch him, and she said could actually feel him!" "Oh, my god!" my brother repeated. I told him about Saje's sister

Serena sitting by Karen Noe on the bus the next day and how she had said, "You can tell a visitation is real when the spirit tells you it is real and asks you to touch them."

"Holy shit!" he exclaimed, "That is just what I remembered! Dad asked me to touch him! He held out his hands to me and told me to touch him. I noticed he had a hole in each of the palms of his hands and so I was a little hesitant to reach out at first. When I finally touched his hand, I could feel him. Then dad said to me, "We are all one in Christ." "Not religiously," my brother added, "Dad told me that we are all one and that's what Christ Consciousness has been trying to teach us. We are always connected and we are all one."

This was a profoundly healing and important experience for my brother, my father, and I. The love, the healing, and the connection continues.

YOUR JOURNEY FORWARD

You can start to connect to that kind of eternal love within you and beyond you now. When you tap into the timeless you can connect with the sublime experience of being alive and to being connected to the Divine in profound ways. You can create your own sacred space to connect with loved ones that have passed and continue the journey together. As you touch into the deeper parts of your being and go beyond the confines of your physical body you can connect with the unending source of love in the universe, the love that goes beyond this life and exists as a constant between and through us all for eternity. You can anchor your soul in the deepest places of peace and begin to befriend it all. It begins with a pause, a deep breath, and touching into your beautiful and radiant heart.

FEELING YOUR CONNECTION

Take a deep breath into your belly and slowly let it go. Take another deep breath in from the souls of your feet and as you exhale feel yourself pushing that breath out of the soles of your feet and down into the earth. Repeat. Then feel the breath come into your body from the tips of your nostrils and feel the coolness of the air as it touches your nostrils. Follow your breath, feeling the sensation in the back of your mouth and throat, and then noticing the rise and fall of your chest with your breath. As you follow the breath down into your belly you can begin to notice the wave of your breath breathing through you.

Then putting a hand on your heart, focus all of your attention on your heartspace and breathe into that. Feel the warmth of your hand on your chest. Feel into your heart, around and through it. Then bring to mind something you are truly grateful for. It doesn't have to be anything big. It can be gratitude for the sun shining or the hot water you showered with today. Allow yourself to move even more deeply to feel the sensation of gratitude radiating through your heart. Allow that glowing energy to penetrate and permeate, go in, around, and through your heart. You will begin to feel a subtle warmth or glow. Breathe into that. Extend the warmth through your heart and imagine it is infusing each and every cell of your being with the radiant light of gratitude.

Now move your attention back into your belly. You can hold your belly with your hands to create even more focus on that area. Extend the love and gratitude from your heart into that space. Feel the movement of your belly and surround it with love. While breathing into this space, extend your awareness into your perineum, or base chakra, and allow yourself to feel it connecting you down into the earth. Feel yourself being truly grounded and rooted to this precious earth that loves, nurtures, and supports you.

Now while staying grounded to the earth, slowly move your attention to the top of your head and to your crown chakra. Start letting that awareness and energy move to six inches above the top of your skull. Imagine the light of the Divine (the universe, or your higher power) streaming down to you. Allow your energy and attention to keep going up, up, up until you feel yourself connect with that light. It can help if you keep your eyes closed, but raise your eyes upwards to bring all of your attention to that connection. Once you feel yourself connected with that energy, allow it to radiate through the column of your being, filling the entirety of you from head to toe and extend the light both above you and below. Keep breathing into this space and tapping in for as long as it feels good to you.

It's okay to start with five minutes and build from there. Doing this practice will allow you to come into more peace with whatever is happening in your life. It will allow you to experience more love and connection, and will foster a knowingness that you are not alone but are intimately connected to a power that transcends circumstances, worries, and fears. Keep practicing daily and be gentle with yourself in the process. Write down the insights and downloads that come through during that time of connection and listen to the inner guidance that is always available to you when you quiet yourself enough to listen.

You are your best guru. All of the answers that you are searching for are right there inside of you. This daily practice will help you find your own truth shining within your sacred soul. In this beautiful mystery of life there are so many things we don't fully understand. You don't have to logically understand "how this all works." That is what faith is about. There are mysteries here that you can begin to only understand in the contents of your heart. The logic of the brain will never master the knowingness of the heart in its infinite wisdom, connected to forces that are stronger than our human minds can imagine.

THE TRUTH IN DREAMS

In a dream I recently had, I was able to pull back the curtain of Oz and see the fabric of what we call our lives, with all of our conditioned thoughts, distractions, and sense of separateness, as all being an illusion. I could see that when we can move past this business and conditioning we are able to move past the need to label things as good or bad, other and self, even darkness and light, and arrive at a place that is total unity beyond it all. It was a place where I could witness the divine play that is the dream of our lives.

In the dream, I remember laughing so hard at the absurdity that we would even consider ourselves separate because we are actually just one being expressing ourselves as trillions of cells, just as we each contain this universe with trillions of cells within us. It became clear that when "we" are in the oneness, it is pure bliss, expansive and wonderful, and the US, that is one, wants to create and experience itself, so it shows up in the form of people, and animals, and wars, and floods, and sunsets… all to experience this diversity and duality as different aspects of the "One."

During the dream, I also kept getting the visualization of honeycombs over and over again as a symbol for how we are all intricately connected and that we may each think we are in an individual cell but we are intimately connected to the entire hive. The image I received was that if one bee was fluttering it's wings, the vibration was felt throughout the whole hive by all and if something happened to one bee, it was felt by the rest of the hive. Each bee was a sacred and intricate part of creating, maintaining, and contributing to the wellness of the community. The same is true of you and me.

Your life is a sacred part of the whole and what you contribute to this world matters. The hive doesn't function the same without you. You are an essential part of the whole. When you are hurting, the ripple is felt by the whole, just as the bees' wings fluttering affects the rest of the hive. When you raise your vibration, like the humming of bees vibrating in unison, it vibrates through the collective consciousness and is felt by the whole hive.

As I continued dreaming, I felt like I was in a sacred school, learning universal lessons that were being given to me from a divine source. I understood that when we want something, it is already in the field of all potentiality so that, as the bible says, we can ask and we shall receive. It became clear that when we are asking for something from a place of abundance, what we are asking for is already given. When asking from a grateful heart and just letting go of the outcome, our wishes are fulfilled. They might not look exactly how we might have planned for them to be, but combined with divine alchemy, they will turn out even better than we could have imagined. In the dream, I was shown that the power of surrender is one of the most powerful forces we have and that when we cling to things having to turn out a certain way we are actually preventing them from happening at all. It is in surrender that we allow for this divine alchemy to occur.

I learned that the things that trigger us in our lives are actually invitations to receive the blessings that lie underneath them and with loving excavation we can help them to heal. It also became clear to me that when things happen that I perceive as being negative (the sickness, the injury, the catastrophe, or the death of someone) they are actually invitations to awaken to higher levels of consciousness. They are the remembrances, like little preset alarms from our soul, inviting us to wake up out of the dream of our lives and awaken to higher levels of consciousness.

We can get caught in the illusions and distractions in life, and sometimes it takes the proverbial two by four to wake us up. I had the thought that if our souls made contracts to come to this earth during this specific time, what if we also contracted to have the things happen to us that appear negative, as wake ups. Just as you would have alarms set on your phone to remind you of things during the day, maybe the "bad" things that happen to us are actually preset reminders that we set up ahead of time to remind us that we can wake up if we choose to. Of course, you or I can press the snooze button. You don't have to wake up when the "alarm" goes off. It is just an opportunity to awaken from the dream. The hope is that we don't sleepwalk through this life. We are essential contributors to this continually unfolding sacred experience.

Very profoundly, I became aware that the words, "Life is but a dream," are not just song lyrics, but the ultimate truth. That life and death are just aspects of one another in the dream of our experience. At one point, I experienced the fear that came from moving through the darkness surrounded by scary, dark images and what felt like a death in my dream, and then something deeper inside of me said, "Just hold on. You know you have to go through the darkness to get to the light." And I did. I experienced waves of rebirth, expansion into bliss and witnessed the cycle of it all. The joy, the tears, the triumphs, the profound pain… I became aware, were all a part of the oneness that is Us.

All the things we go through in our lives and all of the positive and negative things we experience all matter and none of it is personal. There is no God in the sky punishing any of us. Life and death are just aspects and elements of the one dream. You and I experience ourselves in a myriad of ways but are always connected to the whole. All One.

When I awoke, I wrote down as much of this dream as I could remember. It was the most profound dream I had ever experienced and I know there are many pieces that I wish I could recapture and share with you. Maybe in future dreams, more will come (and I will write it all down. I promise.) It felt like such an essential download of truth beyond my knowingness. It reverberated through my cells and felt like all of my cells and my entire being was recalibrating and expanding to realign and vibrate with this greater truth.

WHY IT MATTERS

Why does all of this talking about God, the Divine, and our oneness matter? Why does all of this talking about God, the Divine, and our Oneness matter, and what does it have to do with your big, fat, juicy life? When you embrace that you are a part of the Divine spark of all that is, you begin to connect to the knowingness that your life and your spark will continue. You begin to tap into the sacredness of life more fully knowing that you are a part of this Divine play that is all of our lives and everything around us. When you acknowledge the Divine inside of you and begin looking for it in others, in the rocks, in the trees, in the wind, you will begin to experience life as a hallowed gift, a blessing that is to be shared. You will realize that everything in your life has meaning, every bit of it. The times of trouble and hurting, the elation, the joy, and the challenges are all a part of the same gift. The duality of it all is just a magic dance in the alchemy of the universe. And you, precious dancer, will continue to move in rhythm with the song of eternity as you allow yourself to relax into the knowingness that the song never ends.

When you cling to life or you cling to death it creates suffering. When you come to the understanding that there is no difference between life and death, you can relax into this reverent circle without end. We are all connected, and you are always connected to those you love whether they are living in the physical realm or have transitioned beyond. They are always around you and they are there to provide comfort to you as you navigate through life as things evolve and transform. Life and death are happening around us everywhere, all the time. It is happening to all of us in a very personal way and as a collectively shared experience. As we inhale and exhale, people are dying and others are being born. It is a constant; an underlying rhythm keeping time to the grand melody of the universe. We are all in this eternal dance together.

What kind of power could you tap into if you discovered your soul was truly immortal? How would you show up differently in your community if you knew that we were each powerful healers given the power of love as our most powerful healing balm to share with others and give to ourselves? Imagine the information you could share and receive if you pulled back the curtain and knew beyond a doubt that you had access to all realms of knowledge from both sides.

When you come to peace with death you become an ambassador of peace for the world and can shine your light, illuminating the way for others. When you share your journey and experiences with others, you give them permission to own their own stories and to find their own voice with which to share them as well. We need to share our stories of befriending death, encounters with the Divine, and experiences of connecting with the other side. This is essential knowledge that, when shared, becomes a sacred testimony to the power of the human soul and the eternal depth of love beyond measure.

You, my new dear friend, are a golden thread in this tapestry of humanity that we are all weaving together. It is ok to have differing beliefs, experiences, and ways of being in the world. The essential work is to move beyond our differences to discover the spirit of our souls which are entwined as one, creating the larger body of the universe. As you continue your journey into your deeper relationship with your sacred life and inevitable death, know that you can reach out and you can reach in and connect to the love that transcends death and continues to hold us all eternally.

EMPOWERED

Twenty seven years ago when I started meditating, I had a strong recurring vision that would appear to me at the end of my meditation sessions. It didn't make a lot of sense at the time. I was newly pregnant and my life was flowing quite peacefully. As I reflect on it today, with all the death and violence going on in our world currently, the vision's importance and significance are more apparent to me now. In the vision, I am somewhere in the Middle East and it is desert all around me. I see many men surrounding me, holding what looks like automatic machine guns in their hands. Suddenly, there is a great bright, blinding light on the horizon, and as it emanates down to us, everyone just stops in their tracks. The men are stunned and completely in awe of this radiant light that is surely from the Divine as it shines down on us. As the men focus on the light, they each begin to slowly put down their weapons. They are entranced as they stare in rapture at the light that begins to surround them and then begins to flow into and permeate each and every one of their hearts. The light that is above is suddenly within each one of them, radiating to and through them, connecting them as one. All violence, anger, and fear melted away and all that was left was the illuminated light of love. I pray that this vision becomes a reality. It was so frequent at that point in my life, I can see it now clearly in my mind's eye, as if it were one of my own real memories. It was a vision that clearly said when the light of Divine love flows to us and through us, there will be no more killing and no more cause for death. The power of that love could transform the world and each one of us within it. When we are enveloped by the Divine light of love, we are able to conquer death.

NEXT STEPS

As you are deepening your understanding of death and continued life, are there people you can start having these essential conversations with? Being supported as you continue to awaken can help others to awaken as well. I want to empower you to move more deeply into your heart and to move more deeply into community with others. Together, the great awakening on the planet is possible. You are a spiritual being who is powerful beyond measure. When you share your experiences of life after life and open your heart to hearing the stories from others, you are creating a powerful ripple effect in consciousness. You *are* making a difference. Just like the movement of the bee's wings. Every flutter of your intention is felt by the rest of the hive.

As more and more people do this sacred work, we can come together to create the tipping point in the consciousness of humanity where the veil is lifted and the power of love is what shines through and reveals that we have all been connected and our souls have been immortal the whole time. It is such an exciting time on the planet, even with all the difficulties going on. We are learning how we can transcend them and begin to tap into our soul's potential.

Let this powerful process of befriending the never ending cycle of life begin with your next breath. Yes, this one, in this moment. Breathe into your heart and allow the gorgeous and glorious contents of it to shine through. Know that as you finish this book, you are not alone. Your loved ones beyond the veil are with you, the everlasting Divine spark is within you, and I am right there with you too, offering you a hug from the warmth of my heart to yours.

While we are here on this earth together, we can create a world that honors the individual expression of the Divine that is alive in each one of us. We can touch the timelessness of our souls and allow ourselves to lift the veil that separates us from each other and from those who have passed before us. When you become aware of the Divine spark that radiates through you and never ends, you will begin to see that it resides in and continues in everyone else as well.

The light from our combined sparks illuminates the truth of the one Divine life that is never born and never dies. Take it from the six year old me, or from the stories of the many, many souls who have shared their beautiful experiences here, "Your light continues on." You can live a life free from the fear of death, even when you grieve its arrival. You can more fully savor the moments you are alive and also deeply honor the endings. And one day, the beautiful light that is you will step into eternity, like a blissful and beautiful sunset that in its majesty reminds us, "It is only dark for a little while. It is only dark for a little while. Everything has its sacred time." And the sun, like you, will rise again.

Acknowledgments

First of all, I want to thank Neale Donald Walsch for our beautiful conversation that fateful day in March 2024, that led me to begin this book the next morning. You have changed and inspired my life. A warm thank you to Heather Grey for introducing us.

Much love and gratitude to my amazing literary agent and publisher Lisa Hagan for believing in this book, its message, and its importance in the world.

A deep well of gratitude for my amazing soul sister and phenomenal book coach, Shauna Hardy. I love you with my whole heart. You have been my guiding light for two books and you are absolutely stunning in the perfection of your craft. Thank you for the endless hours of conversations we have shared across the continents making me laugh until I cried so many times! Thank you for believing in me and for seeing the beauty in this book.

Thank you to the many beautiful souls who were interviewed for this book. Love and blessings to you all. Thank you for sharing your truth with us so we all may better be able to speak ours.

So much love to my beautiful friends who have supported me through the journey and have shared the joy of this book coming to fruition. Deep gratitude to the amazing Joy Gribble, whose belief in me and this book provided such an important portal for the last chapter to bloom into being (You are a Rockstar!) A special shout out to the phenomenal Julie Gates- You are my greatest cheerleader and favorite "daily check in" friend. Your love and light have illuminated my darkest moments and our laugh-fests are always one of the best parts of my days. So blessed for our two hour phone calls (that will one day make the BEST podcast!!)

A huge thank you always to my beautiful daughters Acacia Alexandria and Hailey Charlotte. You two are the funniest, brightest, kindest women I know who are both examples of what it means to live authentic lives in full expression. I love you both and adore you endlessly.

Love and deep gratitude to my parents Forrest and Judy, whose unconditional love has held me in the most difficult and joy-filled times of my life and whose belief in me, in all my many expressions, has been unwavering.

And last, but definitely not least, thank you reader, for the gift of your time, and for the joy of your company through these pages. Big love and my deepest gratitude to you.

About the Author

Stephanie James stands at the intersection of personal transformation and spiritual wisdom, weaving together her roles as a transformation coach, psychotherapist, international speaker, filmmaker, and pioneering podcast host. With an innate ability to illuminate the path to authentic self-expression, she has become a trusted voice in the global consciousness movement.

As the creator and host of *Igniting the Spark with Stephanie James*, she engages in profound dialogues with the world's most influential thought leaders, scientists, and spiritual teachers. Her weekly podcast, syndicated worldwide, serves as a beacon for those seeking deeper understanding of psychology, spirituality, and human potential. Through these conversations, Stephanie creates a unique bridge between cutting-edge research and practical wisdom, making transformative insights accessible to audiences worldwide.

Her compelling documentary, *When Sparks Ignite* (currently featured on Humanity Stream+), showcases intimate conversations with renowned international changemakers who reveal how life's greatest challenges can become catalysts for profound transformation. The film masterfully illustrates Stephanie's core message: Our deepest struggles often contain the seeds of our greatest gifts to the world.

In her book, *Becoming Fierce*, Stephanie offers a powerful roadmap for embracing life's full spectrum of experiences. This groundbreaking work guides readers toward embodying their authentic fire—the passionate, purposeful energy that exists within every human being. The book serves as both a practical guide and spiritual companion, teaching readers to love beyond circumstances, live fully present, and express their truest selves as a legacy for future generations.

Drawing from decades of clinical experience and spiritual exploration, Stephanie's approach combines professional expertise with deep emotional wisdom. As a transformation coach and psychotherapist, she has developed a unique methodology that helps individuals not just navigate change, but harness it as a force for personal evolution. Her work provides a clear compass for those seeking to thrive through challenging times, build lasting resilience, and create meaningful change in their lives.

Whether speaking from international stages, facilitating transformative workshops, working one-on-one with clients, or dancing in the kitchen, Stephanie empowers others to discover their internal spark—the authentic core of who they are meant to become. Her message resonates across cultures and demographics, offering a universal invitation to step into a fuller, more empowered expression of self.

Learn more about Stephanie's transformative work at:
https://www.stephaniejames.world

Made in United States
Troutdale, OR
06/22/2025